Able MUSE
A REVIEW OF POETRY, PROSE & ART

NUMBER 18
Winter 2014

www.ablemuse.com

Able Muse Press
publishing the new, the established

Now available from Able Muse Press:

Able Muse Anthology
Edited by Alexander Pepple
Foreword by Timothy Steele

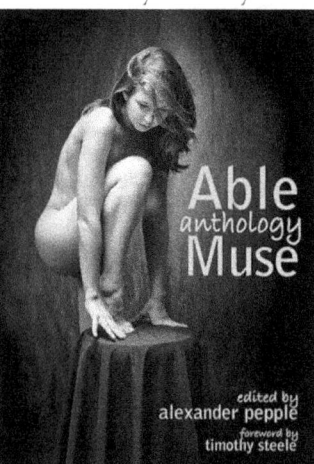

978-0-9865338-0-8 • $16.95

With R.S. Gwynn, Rhina P. Espaillat, Rachel Hadas, Mark Jarman, Timothy Murphy, Dick Davis, A.E. Stallings, Alan Sullivan, Deborah Warren, Diane Thiel, Leslie Monsour, Kevin Durkin, Turner Cassity, Kim Bridgford, Richard Moore and others.

"... Here's a generous serving of the cream of Able Muse including not only formal verse but nonmetrical work that also displays careful craft, memorable fiction (seven remarkable stories), striking artwork and photography, and incisive prose."
— X.J. Kennedy

Able Muse - Inaugural Print Edition

WITH:

POEMS, FICTION, BOOK REVIEWS, INTERVIEWS & ESSAYS from catherine tufariello • catharine savage brosman • leslie monsour • ned balbo • ted mc carthy • diane seuss • susan mclean • rebecca foust • j. patrick lewis • john slater • gail white • kim bridgford • nancy lou canyon • john whitworth • peter filkins • marilyn l. taylor • and others

ISBN 978-0-9865338-2-2

Subscribe to: Able Muse (Print Ed.)

~ Print Edition ~

Semiannual review of poetry, prose & art

Able Muse (Print Edition) continues the excellence in poetry, art, fiction, essays, interviews and book reviews we've brought you all these years in the online edition. Subscribe at *www.ablemusepress.com*

For complete details, visit: **www.AbleMusePress.com**

visit Able Muse

online for more than a decade of archives, plus web-only features not available in the print edition at:

www.ablemuse.com

Able Muse is not just another poetry site. It is one of the best sites on the Internet.
—Heather O'Neil, *Suite101.com*

A forum of Able Muse Review

Able Muse's premier online forums and workshops for metrical and non-metrical poetry, fiction, translations, art, nonfiction and discussions at:

http://eratosphere.ablemuse.com

Able Muse and its extraordinary companion website, the **Eratosphere,** have created a huge and influential virtual literary community. —Dana Gioia

Able Muse
www.ablemuse.com

Editor	Alexander Pepple
Assistant Poetry Editors	Stephen Kampa, Callie Siskel, Reagan Upshaw
Nonfiction Editor	Gregory Dowling
Fiction Editor	Karen Kevorkian
Assistant Fiction Editors	Jonathan Danielson, Janice D. Soderling, Rob Wright
Editorial Board	Rachel Hadas, X.J. Kennedy, A.E. Stallings, Timothy Steele, Deborah Warren

Able Muse is published semiannually. Subscription rates, for individuals: $24.00 per year; libraries and institutions: $34 per year; single and previous issues: $16.95 + $3 S&H. International subscription rates: $33 per year; single and previous issues: $16.95 + $5 S&H. Subscribe online at www.ablemusepress.com or send a check payable to *Able Muse Review* to the snail mail address indicated below. (USD throughout. Online payment with WePay/credit card.)

We read year-round and welcome previously unpublished manuscripts only. No simultaneous submissions. Online or email submissions ONLY. Submission guidelines available at: www.ablemuse.com/submit

Queries and other correspondence should be emailed to: editor@ablemuse.com
For paper correspondence, be sure to include a self-addressed, stamped envelope.

Library of Congress Control Number: 2014919018

ISBN 978-1-927409-47-3 (paperback) / ISBN 978-1-927409-48-0 (digital)

ISSN 2168-0426

Cover image: "Lokbaintan Boat" by Noor Abdillah

Cover & book design by Alexander Pepple

Attn: Alexander Pepple, Editor
Able Muse Review
467 Saratoga Avenue #602
San Jose, CA 95129

www.ablemuse.com
editor@ablemuse.com

Printed in the United States of America
Published in 2014 by Able Muse Press: www.ablemusepress.com

Alexander Pepple

Editorial

Our last issue, the special translation anthology, guest-edited by Charles Martin, has been successfully received and applauded beyond our expectations. To all who wrote, thank you for your kind words. We now return to our regular release schedule, proudly presenting the much anticipated winners of the fourth annual *Able Muse* contests: for the 2014 Able Muse Write Prize, congratulations to Scott M. Miller (for poetry, as selected by final judge Dick Allen) and J. Preston Witt (for fiction, as selected by final judge Amit Majmudar). Kudos also go to the finalists whose work is represented here: Eric Berlin, Catherine Chandler, and Marilyn L. Taylor.

Included in this issue are new poems by our featured poet Wendy Videlock, the first Able Muse Press author to receive this honor. She candidly discusses her poetic craft with interviewer David Mason. Gustavo Thomas is our featured artist, and there is more art and photography from Adel Souto. Additionally, we include our usual complement of new poetry, poetry translations, fiction, essays, interviews, and book reviews from contributors Hailey Leithauser, Jeredith Merrin, Stephen Kampa, Len Krisak, Catharine Savage Brosman, Katharine Coles, Diane Furtney, Hollis Seamon, Martin McGovern, Michael Cohen, N.S. Thompson, Barbara Haas, Derek Furr, Maxine Rosaler, Tamas Dobozy, Michael Lacare, and others.

We also congratulate Carrie Shipers for *Embarking on Catastrophe* and Gail White for *Asperity Street*. They are the winner and runner-up respectively for the 2014 Able Muse Book Award as selected by final judge Molly Peacock. Some of our finalists will, likewise, receive a standard Able Muse Press publication contract. A special thank you to the accomplished poets and writers who participated in our blind reading and shortlisting in the early judging stages.

We have made six nominations for the 2015 Pushcart Prize. These include two poetry translations from the previous issue (X.J. Kennedy's translation from the French of "Evil" by Arthur Rimbaud, and A.E. Stallings's translation from the Greek of "The Five Races of

Man" by Hesiod); two poems from the current issue ("Darning the Wounded Tongue" by Gail Tyson and "The Hermit Convention" by Stephen Kampa); a story from the current issue ("The Tire Swing of Death" by Tamas Dobozy); and an essay from the current issue ("Crucible at Kronshtadt" by Barbara Haas).

Moving along, I am pleased to announce that we are now open for submissions to the 2015 run of *Able Muse* contests. We are honored to have three illustrious final judges: H.L. Hix for the Write Prize for poetry, Eugenia Kim for the Write Prize for fiction; and Peter Campion for the Able Muse Book Award. Entry deadlines are provided in these pages, and details at the Able Muse Press website, www.ablemusepress.com.

Submissions are open year-round for our regular issues, per the guidelines available online at www.ablemuse.com/submit/.

Able Muse Press has been busy with the release of new books of poetry, including *All the Wasted Beauty of the World,* the third full-length collection from Richard Newman (finalist for the 2012 Able Muse Book Award). We also have releases from the 2013 Able Muse Book Award: *Cup,* the third full-length collection from special honoree Jeredith Merrin; the first full-length collections from finalists Chelsea Woodard and D.R. Goodman, *Vellum* and *Greed: A Confession* respectively; and the winning collection *Walking in on People* by Melissa Balmain.

We welcome our new assistant editors Stephen Kampa and Callie Siskel for poetry, and Jonathan Danielson for fiction. We offer thanks to our departing assistant editors (Peter Austin, poetry, and John Riley, fiction), as well as to our returning editors (Karen Kevorkian, fiction, and Gregory Dowling, nonfiction), and assistant editors (Janice D. Soderling and Rob Wright, fiction, and Reagan Upshaw, poetry).

We appreciate your continued support of *Able Muse* and Able Muse Press, and hope you'll enjoy this issue as much as we've enjoyed bringing it to you.

The very best,

Alexander Pepple
—Editor

BOOKS
FROM
ABLE MUSE PRESS

NEW & RECENT RELEASES

MELISSA BALMAIN:
Walking in on People – Poems
~ WINNER, 2013 ABLE MUSE BOOK AWARD ~

JEREDITH MERRIN: *Cup – Poems*
~ SPECIAL HONOREE, 2013 ABLE MUSE BOOK AWARD ~

CHELSEA WOODARD: *Vellum – Poems*

D.R. GOODMAN:
Greed: A Confession – Poems

RICHARD NEWMAN:
All the Wasted Beauty of the World – Poems

ELLEN KAUFMAN: *House Music – Poems*

BARBARA ELLEN SORENSEN: *Compositions of the Dead Playing Flutes – Poems*

FRANK OSEN: *Virtue, Big as Sin – Poems*
~ WINNER, 2012 ABLE MUSE BOOK AWARD ~

JAMES POLLOCK: *Sailing to Babylon – Poems*

MATTHEW BUCKLEY SMITH:
Dirge for an Imaginary World – Poems
~ WINNER, 2011 ABLE MUSE BOOK AWARD ~

APRIL LINDNER:
This Bed Our Bodies Shaped – Poems

RICHARD WAKEFIELD: *A Vertical Mile – Poems*

HOLLIS SEAMON:
Corporeality – Stories

CAROL LIGHT:
Heaven from Steam – Poems

STEPHEN SCAER:
Pumpkin Chucking – Poems

MARYANN CORBETT: *Credo for the Checkout Line in Winter – Poems*

WENDY VIDELOCK:
The Dark Gnu and Other Poems

BEN BERMAN:
Strange Borderlands – Poems

CATHERINE CHANDLER:
Lines of Flight – Poems

MARGARET ANN GRIFFITHS:
*Grasshopper:
The Poetry of M A Griffiths*

WENDY VIDELOCK:
Nevertheless – Poems

AARON POOCHIGIAN:
The Cosmic Purr – Poems

MICHAEL CANTOR:
Life in the Second Circle – Poems

LATEST ABLE MUSE PRESS CATALOG
Free Download at: www.ablemusepress.com/catalog

2015 Able Muse Write Prize
for poetry & fiction

» **$500 prize** for the poetry winner
  » *All poetry styles welcome (metrical & free verse)*

» **$500 prize** for the fiction winner

» plus, **publication** in Able Muse (Print Edition)

» **Blind judging** by the final judges

» **Final Judges**: H.L. Hix (poetry);
  Eugenia Kim (fiction)

» **Entry Deadline:** February 15, 2015

**GUIDELINES & ENTRY INFORMATION
AVAILABLE ONLINE AT:**

www.ablemusepress.com

2015 Able Muse Book Award
for poetry

» **$1000 prize** *for winning manuscript, plus*

» **publication** *by Able Muse Press*

» *All poetry styles welcome (metrical & free verse)*

» **Blind judging** *by the final judge*

» *Final Judge: Peter Campion*

» *Entry Deadline:* March 31, 2015

**GUIDELINES & ENTRY INFORMATION
AVAILABLE ONLINE AT:**

www.ablemusepress.com

CONTENTS

Alexander Pepple
    EDITORIAL / *v*

ESSAYS

N.S. Thompson
    READING DONALD JUSTICE'S
        "LORCA IN CALIFORNIA" / *81*

Michael Cohen
    THE PLACE WHERE IT HAPPENED / *100*

Barbara Haas
    CRUCIBLE AT KRONSHTADT / *119*

Derek Furr
    OUR ELIZABETH, WALCOTT MINE / *178*

INTERVIEWS

R.S. Gwynn
    INTERVIEWED BY JASON PHILLIP REESER / *88*

FEATURED POET

Wendy Videlock
    A MOONWALK IN A COWBOY HAT: AN INTERVIEW BY DAVID MASON / *139*

    POEMS

        THESE ARE THE THINGS I THINK I KNOW: / *153*

        THE VIGILANTES / *154*

        INVOCATION / *155*

        WHAT THE SCULPTOR SAID / *156*

        IN THE WIND / *157*

ART & PHOTOGRAPHY

Adel Souto
- Photography / *96*
- ARTWORK
  - Cleopatra's Needle / *97*
  - Walk on by / *98*
  - Ride the island / *99*

FEATURED ARTIST

Gustavo Thomas
- A Photographic Exhibit / *107*
- ARTWORK
  - A walker in Central Park / *108*
  - One one line, one one foot / *109*
  - Peggy's Cove BNW panorama / *111*
  - Figure near Sólfar / *112*
  - On the bridge / *113*
  - National Monument of Scotland / *114*
  - Harmony / *115*
  - The Egg / *116*
  - Water Street (Osaka) / *117*
  - Sensō-ji During Sanja Matsuri / *118*

2014 Write Prize for Poetry • Winner

Scott M. Miller
- Costanza e Preziosa / *58*

2014 Write Prize for Poetry • Finalists

Eric Berlin
- For Lack of What Is Found / *80*

Catherine Chandler
- Discovery / *168*

Marilyn L. Taylor
- River II: Accidental Reflection / *127*

POETRY

Lisa Huffaker
　Wake / 1

Gail Tyson
　Harvest / 2
　Darning the Wounded Tongue / 4

Stephen Kampa
　The Hermit Convention / 6

Judith Kunst
　Like Nothing Ever Seen on Earth / 9

Paul Verlaine
(translated by Diane Furtney)
　A Woman and Her Cat / 23

Teresa Milbrodt
　The Passion of Jude / 25

Peter Austin
　Twenty Years On / 26

Kyle Potvin
　To My Children Reading
　　My Poetry after I'm Gone / 40

Len Krisak
　Trees in November / 41

Susan McLean
　Short-Timer / 42

Roy Bentley
　"Squirrels on Skis"
　　Star Performer Dies / 45

Jeredith Merrin
　The Burrowing Owl / 47
　The Pharaoh Eagle Owl / 50

Hailey Leithauser
　Rrribbit / 51
　Sour Grapes / 52
　Triolet with Typewriter / 53
　The Hangman's Song / 54

Pierre de Ronsard
(translated by Terese Coe)
　Challenge for a Mounted
　　Tournament in the Form
　　of a Ballet / 55

Frank De Canio
　Tough Customer / 57

Dorie deWitt LaRue
　To the Young Muslim Woman
　　in Full Niqab on Motorcycle / 70

Kathryn Locey
　New Wine / 72

Katharine Coles
　Either They Were Human / 74

Catharine Savage Brosman
　Departure / 76
　Sunny / 78

J.P. Grasser
　Gyroscope / 128

Zara Raab
> The Sere, the Yellow Leaf / 129

Robert W. Crawford
> Calypso Calls on Penelope / 163

Duane Caylor
> Cicero Comments / 164

Anne-Marie Thompson
> Sonnet / 170

FICTION

Tamas Dobozy
> The Tire Swing of Death / 11

Maxine Rosaler
> The Uncle / 27

Michael Lacare
> Claire / 60

Bridget Apfeld
> Water Deep, Cold / 130

Anthony Mastroianni
> Midnight in Paris / 158

2014 Write Prize for Fiction • Winner

J. Preston Witt
> Lesson One / 43

BOOK REVIEWS

Martin McGovern
> Three Reviews:
>> Stephen Kampa,
>> *Bachelor Pad* / 171
>>
>> Quincy R. Lehr,
>> *Heimat: A Poem* / 171
>>
>> Joshua Mehigan,
>> *Accepting the Disaster* / 171

Hollis Seamon
> Eight Stories In Search of an Editor:
>> A Review of Jacob M. Appel,
>> *Scouting for the Reaper* / 187

CONTRIBUTOR NOTES / 199

INDEX / 209

Congratulations to the 2014 *Able* MUSE CONTEST WINNERS

2014 ABLE MUSE WRITE PRIZE

FICTION
Final Judge: **Amit Majmudar**

WINNER
J. Preston Witt
"Lesson One"

HONORABLE MENTION
Andrea Witzke Slot

POETRY
Final Judge: **Dick Allen**

WINNER
Scott M. Miller
"Costanza e Preziosa"

FINALISTS
Eric Berlin:
"For Lack of What Is Found"

Catherine Chandler: "Discovery"

Marilyn L. Taylor:
"River II: Accidental Reflection"

SHORTLIST
- Eric Berlin (twice) • David Culwell
- William E. Rogers (twice) • Safiya Sinclair (twice) • David Southward

2014 ABLE MUSE BOOK AWARD

POETRY MANUSCRIPT
Final Judge: **Molly Peacock**

WINNER
Carrie Shipers
Embarking on Catastrophe

SECOND PLACE
Gail White
Asperity Street

SHORTLIST
- Clayton Adam Clark: *Strange Commerce*
- William Cordeiro: *Trap Street*
- Heidi Czerwiec: *Song Against Songs*
- Midge Goldberg: *The Snowman's Code*
- Sarah Grieve: *Dear Dr. Frankenstein*
- Patricia Hooper: *Separate Flights*
- Richard Meyer: *Shooting Stars*
- Carolyn Raphael: *Dancing with Bare Feet*
- William Craig Rice: *New Old Stock (NOS) - Sonnets & Other Verse*

BOOKS FROM SOME OF THE SHORTLISTED AUTHORS ALSO COMING SOON FROM ABLE MUSE PRESS!

Walking in on People
Poems
by Melissa Balmain

*NEW~ from Able Muse Press

WINNER
2013 Able Muse Book Award

PRAISE FOR *WALKING IN ON PEOPLE*
(with an foreword by David Yezzi)

The first full-length collection from Melissa Balmain

★★★★★

"Balmain's poems add to the rhythmic bounce of light verse a darker, more cutting humor."
— Billy Collins, former Poet Laureate of the US

"*Walking in on People* grabbed me with its very title, and it never let go . . . [Melissa Balmain] really commands her art."
— X.J. Kennedy (Judge, 2013 Able Muse Book Award)

"So many of the poems in Melissa Balmain's triumphant debut lodge themselves in that Frostian zone where they are hard to get rid of."
— David Yezzi (from the foreword)

ISBN 978-1-927409-29-9 / 102 pages
ORDER NOW FROM ABLE MUSE PRESS AT: WWW.ABLEMUSEPRESS.COM
OR, ORDER FROM AMAZON.COM, BN.COM & OTHER ONLINE OR OFFLINE BOOKSTORES

www.AbleMusePress.com

Lisa Huffaker

Wake

What absence means depends on what is gone,
what's missing; but the figure of its wake
depends on what is left to carry on.

And though the boat itself, once it has drawn
its slashing silver line across a lake,
is absent, something's left to show it's gone.

That bright wound on the water hails the dawn
of *afterwards,* delineates the break
between *before* and what must carry on.

As water curls to seal the slit upon
its face, does that effacement then unmake
its meaning? That depends. What's gone is gone;

once absence and its freight have undergone
their exile, nothing's left that can forsake
whatever must remain to carry on;

but here's the line that cannot be withdrawn:
a rippling gash, all silver and opaque.
Your absence hoards its meaning. You are gone,
and that is what goes on and on and on.

Gail Tyson

Harvest

I.

This work takes steady hands:
The first cut into still
warm flesh, the incision
wishbone-shaped though the luck
is yours, not his, then hours
of severing bile ducts,
veins, arteries until,
regal as a priestess,
your surgeon elevates
the liver. She divines
your future in his death,
places this amulet
inside you while you sleep.
Later you wake, hear, weep.

II.

Elsewhere, these harvests
are big business. Prisoners,
the homeless, the challenged
wake without a kidney,
or don't, if traffickers
score a liver or heart.
When global markets crashed
the organ trade boomed.
Another crash, head-on
claimed the boy, gave meaning
to the sacrifice—"made
holy, made whole"—that called
you to higher ground:
a Cosmic Lost and Found.

III.

The transplant has taught you
why Harvest is its own
season, distinct from Fall,
how the best offering
you can make is simply
thanks. Your gratitude tends
the life planted in you,
a child's liver now grown
to serve your middle age.
Thanks is a way to hold
steady, to lift up his
spirit, make this autumn
of your life a votive.

Gail Tyson

Darning the Wounded Tongue

Half-dog, half-camel, with bottomless eyes,
the creature kneels beside me like a sphinx.
Erect, tall in a Queen Anne chair, I gaze
ahead. Neither of us makes a sound.

The creature kneels beside me in a pale room,
silvery light casting peace around us.
Neither of us makes a sound. She opens
her mouth, revealing one wound on her tongue.

The light casts peace as evenly as stitches
lined up on a needle, its long arc
revealing a deep wound on her tongue; it
isn't bleeding. I pick up fine white yarn

and needle—a long arc hovering, silent,
above the deep, oval wound, which is not
bleeding but yearning for the fine white yarn.
Slowly I begin to sew it up.

The oval hole, deep as the brown eyes trained
on me, accepts my stitches, unflinching.
Sewing up the gaping wound, I'm relieved
these sutures do not hurt. As I sew and

sew without flinching, without ceasing
the ancient rhythm seems to heal me, too.
Thankful that these sutures do not hurt,
I sense an old truth rising from our bond

just before waking, as if the creature
testifies: The world can be mended.

Stephen Kampa

The Hermit Convention

From WiFi basements, caves and trailer parks,
Down from their stylish pillars, out of the blue,
The hermits are arriving. Sure enough,
    At first they have to suffer
Through frigid icebreakers, silence, and a few
    Rebarbative remarks
From mossy-bearded bards with halitosis;
But after lunch, the t-shirt free-for-all,
    And some judicious doses
Of welcome Johnnie Walker (neat), the ball

Starts rolling. Wandering ascetics jog
In groups, comparing orthopedic soles;
Recluses swap their locust recipes;
    The tech-teens dub the "geezers"
"More antiquated than piano rolls,"
    Then cringe to find the blog
They all adore is written by the oldest.
Some conferees seem hitherto unknown:
    The pouting centerfold,
The full-time dad, the addict, each alone

In ways so daring they're the avant-garde
Of hermithood, according to the scholars
(Much in attendance). "Inner solitude,"
     One specialist concluded,
"Will be pursued through paparazzi hollers,
     Kids' tantrums in the yard,
And needles. What are mountain mists compared
To mental fogs? Or crystal streams to crack?"
     (None of the hermits cared
For what he said; they won't invite him back.)

Day One, they're usually too tired to flirt,
But come Day Two, the random footsie starts.
Day Three: the hook-ups, hang-ups, downward spirals.
     Day Four: hair-shirts. They tie
Their tunics' simple knots, they cinch their hearts
     And cover their faces with dirt,
And after several hours of this, they're sure
The whole deal smacks of fate, that they were driven
     To something this impure
So they remember how to be forgiven.

Clearly some come who can't be satisfied.
The largest rooms feel crowded, food's no good,
Not all participants have taken vows
      (Cf. Day Three's carousing),
Beds are too soft—these folks take hermithood
      Seriously, with pride.
They are the ones who know an anchor-hold
Was sealed up brick by brick, extemporize
      On "years of bitter cold"—
It's them the other hermits ostracize.

Everyone leaves one weekend, still unkempt
But slightly less so. Some exchange addresses,
Believing letters won't defile their silence
      Because they won't reply.
The last to go survey the modest mess:
      A deck of cards, an empty
Beer bottle, trampled grass, an unlatched gate.
A hermit thrush—where?—flutes as the whole brood
      Retreats to contemplate
Their solidarity in solitude.

Judith Kunst

Like Nothing Ever Seen on Earth

First thing you'll be amazed at is your mama
flying the high trapeze, her long hair streaming
scarlet curlicues. The only time your papa

fumbles his top-hat words is when she's beaming
at him from the hammock where she tumbles
in the grand finale. He's nervous, dreaming

you'll be frightened by the big top, its rumbles
of tigers and applause. But I'm guessing
you'll get used to all the bells and drumrolls

pretty quickly. We clowns will want help pressing
cream pies to our faces; you can try on
my fake nose, or tickle me while I'm dressing

for the encores. There's a golden lion
who means to greet you when you're older,
and monkeys who'll teach you how to climb on

the rafters. Then the weather will get colder.
We'll lower the long poles and fold up the tents.
We'll hoist the magic carpets on our shoulders.

You'll walk in front, between the elephants,
where you can see the new road winding down.
To the sky, you can practice your "Ladies and gents!"
while I plaster the ads in the next town.

FICTION

Tamas Dobozy
The Tire Swing of Death

On the day I was fired from Nolan Incorporated, Benjamin had this idea: he'd sit on one of the tire swings in our backyard, swinging around and around in circles, while I swung the other one at him, trying to knock him off. Then he'd post the video on YouTube. It was a typical Benjamin idea—dangerous and idiotic—and the more he hurt himself, falling off and slamming into the ground, the harder he'd laugh, and the more Marcy and me would look at each other and wonder, what's with this kid?

I'd just come home from the office—old Bartholomew Nolan made sure I put in a full day before handing me my pink slip—and was standing out there in my suit, shivering in the early spring, water seeping up around my oxfords, holding the tire and thinking: What kind of father tries to make his son fall off a swing? And who's going to watch this video? Not just Benjamin's friends, I guessed, and possibly their parents, though they knew Benjamin well enough not to be alarmed, but also complete strangers, and who knew what kind of conclusions they'd come to? That my son was maybe mental, and I was taking advantage of his condition to create a new backyard sport? Let's get together guys, grab some beers, and take shots at my deranged kid on the tire swing. And you can each pay me ten bucks a shot, because I'm unemployed.

Benjamin was setting up the camera to record video when I called out to him: "Hey, can you at least get me a mask from the costume box?"

"Why, Dad?"

"Uh, it'll look cooler."

"Well, which mask? Superhero? Something else?"

"It doesn't matter. Any mask."

He ran in and came out smiling a minute later, holding the skeleton face he'd worn when dressed as the Grim Reaper the Halloween before. I put it on thinking it probably looked pretty good with the suit. Death wears Hugo Boss. No fucking around.

"Okay, Dad," he said, hitting the button on the camera balanced on the railing of our back porch, and taking a running leap at the tire swing. I took aim, trying to predict his arc, and gave the tire a good push. It missed once, swung back, missed again, Benjamin laughing, and then, most of its momentum spent, finally connected, Benjamin losing his grip on purpose, falling to the ground, lying there as if he was dead. "Let's get another take," he said, getting up after a while, one side caked in mud.

I itched my nose under the skull mask. "Right," I said. And we did it again.

Well, the video was a hit. "The Tire Swing of Death," Benjamin called it, and based on the viewers' comments it was Death himself (me, in other words) who was the star of the show. "Dude, your dad looks awesome," his friend, Will, wrote. "Epic duds, Death," wrote Travis, another friend. "It would be cooler if, like, Death stabbed you with his scythe after you fell off the tire swing," wrote Markus.

I looked at the comments wondering if that should be my next career move. I still hadn't told anyone I'd been fired, neither the kids, nor my wife, Marcy, and was counting on the severance package to last until the next job came along, though it needed to come along quick. Things weren't great in our house then. We had four young children, Marcy didn't work, and the stress she felt, being with the kids all day, and up with them much of the night, and then me coming home from a bad day at the office into a house that was twice as much work, was cracking our marriage in too many places to count. The last thing Marcy needed to hear—on top of the dirty diapers (Molly and Lucy were two), and chronic ear and lung infections (like many twins they'd been born premature, with all the medical complications that entails), and sleepless nights (because of the pain); on top of our guilt over Henry (who was four) being sidelined by the attention the girls demanded; on top of Benjamin's death-defying stunts (it seemed like we had to spend seven hours in emergency with him at least one night every few weeks) and reluctance to do homework or eat dinner or get dressed or go to bed when asked or stop telling us everything that happened to be running through his mind at any given moment (even while the girls were screaming for attention, and Henry trying to get in a word); and on top of the fact that we couldn't afford the babysitting we needed just to get a night off to regroup, and that our house was too small, with the girls crammed into one room, Henry relocated to a walk-in closet, and Benjamin sleeping in the basement guest suite—on top of all that the last thing she needed to hear was that we were destitute. So I was pretending to go to work every morning, wandering the streets, drinking at crappy coffee shops, then coming home and pretending at night to be sorting my briefcase, shuffling papers, doing spreadsheets on the laptop I was waiting for Nolan Incorporated to notice I hadn't yet returned.

So Benjamin's *Death Suite* of videos was a welcome distraction. The truth is, the relationship between my eldest son and me had at its core an ecstatic violence, like the time I attached a pulley high in a tree, then pulled him up and down it in an old trunk until one day I fumbled the rope and he crashed down; or the time we played the game where he'd take a flying leap onto me from the bed, with each jump I'd move a little further away, until I realized he wasn't going to make it and reached to catch him and our heads came together with a brain-jarring crunch; or the time he practiced sneak attacks—like in the *Pink Panther* movie where Clouseau is randomly assaulted by his servant, Kato—jumping from behind doors, closets, corners, and punching me in the gut, to which I'd respond with a grunt, "You can't hurt steel," and then turn and try not to heave.

But the videos, they were different. The *Death Suite* wasn't just fun, it had an *aesthetic*. The films were all Benjamin's idea. There was "Death Goes Tubing," where I put on my swim shorts, grabbed an overinflated inner tube, put on the mask, and rode the rapids along Grand River, with Benjamin running on the bank filming me along the same thirty foot stretch until he had enough material. There was "Death the Babysitter," where I ran after Molly and Lucy while they scampered in diapers back and forth along our second floor hallway. There was "Death Tries to Eat," where I lifted various kinds of food—cereal, apples, a hot dog, potato chips—and crushed them into the plastic teeth at the front of the mask, milk and fruit and meat dribbling off the skull onto the front of my shirt, the scene ending with me sobbing in front of a blackberry pie as if Death had realized that no matter what he did he'd never get born, never get to smell spring on the breeze, feel summer on his skin, enjoy the taste of baked berries.

But one day while we were filming "Death the Shredder?" the skateboard slipped out from under me, and I went skidding down Chicopee Hill on my ass. My neighbor, Cheryl Gainsley, was waiting at the bottom, standing at the end of her driveway. By the time she'd helped me up, Benjamin had skated down as well, camera still in hand.

"Nice mask," she said. "Is that a skateboarder thing?"

I went to take it off, but Benjamin yelled out, "Dad, I'm still filming."

"Tell me, Death," Cheryl laughed, "when are you coming for me?"

"I don't think that's a good thing to joke about, if you . . ."

"Tell her," Benjamin said.

"Tuesday," I quickly said, and Cheryl and I both smiled. "You'll be hit by a chunk of fuselage falling from a disintegrating airplane."

"Thanks!" she said. "I'll make sure to remember my umbrella when I go out."

On the walk home, Benjamin said the umbrella comment reminded him of those cartoons where the Coyote has once again screwed up his death trap and the boulder or cannonball or anvil that's supposed to have fallen on the Road Runner is instead falling on him, and he puts up a little pink umbrella as the shadow of his impending doom grows larger and larger around him until wham! he's pulverized beneath it.

That Tuesday, Cheryl Gainsley was severely injured when the guy topping her maples made the wrong crosscut, and she was driven into the ground where she'd been standing by a ton of falling treetop.

She didn't die, but Benjamin was stunned. "It's just like you predicted."

Before his mother could cut him off for talking nonsense, I said, "What are you saying? It's not even close. I said she'd be hit by a fuselage, and that she'd die."

"She almost *did* die," Marcy chimed in.

"Not by a fuselage," I countered. I couldn't believe we were now debating the fine points, as if there was something in all of this.

"We just need to dial in a bit," Benjamin muttered. "If instead of fuselage you'd said, 'A big thing will fall on you from the sky,' you would have been right!" I looked at him, trying to decide if he was serious, thinking of how "Death the Shredder?" would play on YouTube for Cheryl's family, and then an image flashed into my mind of Benjamin in front of a big radio, the old-fashioned kind, polished ebony, kneeling on the floor with his ear to the speaker and twisting the knob along miles of static until he came to the one station receiving, pressing in his ear to catch the whisper. I shuddered and shook my head. "What I mean," he said, "is you could use it to send positive messages."

"There's nothing to use, Benj," I said. "It was just a coincidence, and anyhow you're the one who made me say it."

He'd do it again, days later. We were at his friend's place, a kid by the name of Markus with whom Benjamin had the kind of love/hate relationship that's only possible when you're young or married. Naturally, I wore the skull mask, and was sitting with Markus's parents, Cindy and Greg, who were trying not to giggle, to look as serious and concerned as Benjamin had directed, though Markus was staring up at me like he'd lost all respect. This episode was called, "Death Schedules a Parent/Teacher Conference."

"So, you're saying my son will be a great man?" Cindy said, trying to keep her eyes from flickering at the bits of script Benjamin's younger brother, Henry (being paid for his work in chocolate bars), was holding up for us to read.

"Yes, but first he will fail his math test."

"The one next week?" Greg asked.

"The one next week," I said.

"But that's an important one," Cindy said.

"There's no way I'm failing that test," Markus said to his parents, who tried not to laugh, so secure were they in their son's ability to beat my son, every time, on every single test, mental or physical, though the truth is the boys were always close, Markus edging Benjamin by so little it was a question of confidence rather than aptitude.

"Worse than that," I said, "is that the failure will precipitate his general decline." It took me a long time to get the lines out. "General decline," I continued, "from the heights of academe, into, as it were, the world of common men. But do not fear, he will rise from this, in time, and renewed and strengthened, will mount to the absolute heights." I pulled off the mask and looked at Benjamin. "There's no way Death would talk like this!" I said. "It's too fancy." Until now, I'd been playing Death as a no-bullshit guy.

"Stop being like Marlon Brando," Benjamin said, "just read your lines."

Cindy and Greg burst out laughing.

It was only later that week, following a hunch, going through our Netflix history, that I realized how many movies Benjamin had been watching, late at night, while he was supposed to be asleep: *On the Waterfront, Last Tango in Paris, Apocalypse Now.* There was no way he should be watching movies like those, and when I told Marcy she was horrified. "Get the butter," she said, and we both closed our eyes and winced.

But that conversation was lost in the blow up around Markus failing the math test, and the fit he had afterwards, throwing down the paper and pointing a finger at Benjamin and saying he planned it all with that movie of his, to which Benjamin replied, "Don't blame me if you suck at math," at which point Markus jumped on him, someone ran to get the principal, who got a bloody nose trying to separate them, and now there was a suspension, talk of expelling Markus, plus Cindy giving Marcy the cold shoulder at the grocery store, and Greg phoning me to say we'd better not post that video.

"Nice work, Dad," said Benjamin, laughing. "I finally beat Markus on a test."

"You had this planned, didn't you?"

"He's fragile," Benjamin shrugged. "People with big egos usually are."

"You're supposed to be his friend," I said.

"Sometimes we're friends," he replied.

I watched his face carefully as he spoke, another instance of that sick fascination you get watching your child's inner world emerge, the troubles that rise and consume his thoughts as time goes by, less easy to ignore as the rush of curiosity and energy and eagerness that is childhood fades. He was unhappy with Markus, and unhappy with himself for that unhappiness, and I could see him struggling to make both feelings go away, just as I struggled in those days, sitting on the floor of the bathroom dressing the girls after their bath, trying not to think of how I'd lost my job, of my family being out in the cold, my brain warping these worries into fantasies I couldn't shake, where at any minute the girls were going to be teleported off the bathroom floor into some cold place, maybe eight or ten degrees, warm enough for them to survive provided I could get their clothes on in time—their diapers, their onesies, their socks, their pajamas—my fingers fumbling with the snaps, trying to get their arms and legs in, thinking that with each successful article of clothing they were one step closer to survival, they'd last that much longer, though it was distressing to think that Lucy was dressed, so she'd certainly make it, but Molly was only half-dressed, so she'd sit there, in that cold place, slowly freezing to death while Lucy looked at her, unable to figure out what was wrong, too young to realize she could save her sister by warming her until help showed. The fantasies also happened while I was making lunches for the boys, standing in the kitchen playing out more or less the same scenario, except that in this case the boys would be teleported to some place where there was no food, nothing to eat except for what I'd managed to pack before time ran out, and which would magically reappear for them in their lunchboxes every day, that and nothing else, so I'd find myself bustling around the kitchen trying to get as many things into their lunches as quickly as I could, thinking, Well, at least they'll have an apple, or, Now they'll have an apple plus cookies, or, Now they'll have an apple plus cookies plus some carrots, all the way through until I had the sandwiches and drinks in there, at which point I'd relax and think, Okay, they'll probably be able to live on that, it's enough food to keep them going until I can find out where they've been teleported to and rescue them. The fantasies were crazy but unstoppable, domestic death rituals, and I blamed it on losing my job instead of blaming it, as I should have, on the mask.

I thought that business with Markus would be the end of the *Death Suite,* but it was just the start. Because even though Benjamin never again asked me to put on the mask—sensing our anger in the cancellation of the Netflix account—he was still spreading the word. Either that, or people had found out about what had happened to Cheryl and Markus, maybe through YouTube, where Benjamin, before we told him to take it down, had posted "Death Schedules a Parent/Teacher Conference" after all, like some gladiator having one last laugh at a crushed enemy. That Monday, when I got home from my hopeless job search, Marcy reminded me of the surprise retirement party that had been planned months ago for old Bartholomew Nolan, and which I'd totally forgotten about. Had I remembered, I might have faked sickness or come up with some other reason why we couldn't make it, but now I either had to go, and hope no one mentioned me being fired (and why would they when it would just cause everyone embarrassment, not to mention ruin Bart's retirement party?), or come clean and tell Marcy what had happened. I decided to go. I wanted to see the discomfort on Bart's lizard face.

I would regret that decision the minute Marcy and I walked into the "parties and banquet" room at the Waterloo Recreation Centre and Wally Bifford came up to me and handed over the mask with a laugh, saying I should really say a few words about what was waiting for old Bart down the road in retirement. Marcy and I stood there, the only ones not laughing. The mask was exactly like the one we had at home, and I realized that everyone at work must have watched Benjamin's videos.

Wally pretended it was joke, but there was something serious in the way he said, "Nolan Incorporated stock options, up or down?" I stood there holding the mask, flapping it in my hand, not wanting to put it on, realizing that Wally and everyone else didn't care one iota about Bart and his retirement. What they cared about was the fact that I'd been fired, along with a number of other people, and how odd it was that old Bart was retiring when he was still on top of the game, and whether they should cash out their Nolan Incorporated options or maybe even start looking for new jobs.

"Very funny," I said.

"C'mon, make a prediction," Wally replied, faking another laugh.

"Death the Financial Advisor" Evelyn Spratly said, pulling out her iPhone and turning the camera on me. "Aaaaaaaand action!" she howled.

"We want Death! We want Death! We want Death!" Everyone was chanting.

Reluctantly I put it on. What would Benjamin want me to say at a moment like this? "Money will be of no significance to Bart," I started, with no idea where the words were coming from, and images, too, like there was a documentary, complete with voice-over, running through my head. "Though we know him for his . . . thrift," I continued, "things will change rapidly in the days to come." It felt like the mask was talking. "Bart will come to face, as we all must face, the great nothingness." I tore off the mask and stared at it, but it was too late, the damage had been done, everyone, especially Bart, was staring at me, the room silent except for the corny 1930s jazz playing in the background.

Marcy took my arm and got me out of there. "What are you doing?" she said in the car, sitting behind the driver's wheel while I stared at the mask, almost overcome by the urge, believe it or not, to put it back on again.

"It was there," I said. "It was there in my mind." I didn't know what else to say, and I knew, even that night I knew, in the midst of the absurdity of my performance, that we'd be getting news two weeks after about how Bartholomew Nolan had climbed out the window of his penthouse apartment, nailed the end of his Turnbull and Asser tie to the ledge, and leapt into space only to slam back against the wall of the apartment, dangling there like some victim of his own dress code. He'd always insisted that the men working for him wear a necktie every day, no exceptions, including the time he'd sent Jerry Aschenbach home from a meeting for not having one.

The night after Bart died our phone would not stop ringing. It seemed I was running to pick it up every ten minutes, listening to traumatized ex-colleagues calling to ask if I was happy, having said those horrible things to Bart at his retirement party, as if I hadn't predicted his death so much as inspired it. Had they forgotten that Bart had fired me? Had they forgotten the newspaper reports that said Bart was bankrupt—old arch-conservative Bartholomew Nolan up to his carefully groomed head in debt—with some reports citing gambling, prostitutes, drugs, and that his "retirement" had not at all been voluntary, with the board of directors telling him he'd either have to go quietly or be thrown out on his ass, the whole thing kept secret so Bart could save face, except for the fact that he hadn't, in the end, been able to do it—go quietly.

The phone calls that disturbed me the most were Wally Bifford's, getting in touch to say the new owners had moved quickly to reorganize the company, that he'd been given a promotion to senior director and additional "head count" for his team, and he'd be only too happy to hire me back if I promised to give him "tips in the way of world events, particularly those that might affect daily fluctuations in the sale of commodities."

It was after the fifth such call, with me seriously thinking of taking up Wally's offer—which would more or less have meant wearing the mask to work—when the police showed up wondering if I'd be able to answer a few questions.

Not wanting to disturb the kids I left Marcy to answer the phone and went out with them onto the front steps. They asked to see the mask, and I went back inside and got it. The cops passed it back and forth. One of them even tried it on briefly. "You had no idea Mr. Nolan might be suicidal? Were you anywhere near him on the night of his death? Did you ever have any conflicts of a personal nature with Mr. Nolan, either on or off the job—I mean before he fired you?"

I barely knew Bartholomew Nolan. He was too high above me, though once in a while he'd come down from his office and stroll through the ranks as he'd probably been trained to do at some management seminar, looking over shoulders, asking basic questions of working groups, giving someone a pat on a back or one of those looks that said you better get back to work. But the cops didn't look convinced when I told them this, staring at me under their eyebrows as if no one who'd said what I said at the retirement party could have such a distant relationship.

"Can you put on the mask?" one of the cops asked. I looked at him like he was crazy. "Please put on the mask," he said, his tone harsher. And once I did, he said, "Look at me and tell me what you see."

It took less than a minute for the movie to come on in my head, that bad parade of images, and what they showed took all my energy not to repeat, though the mask felt glued to my face now, its lipless mouth melded to mine, insisting I put words to all that it was showing me. I was in a sweat, trying to maintain control. "I see prosperity," I said, feeling as if the mask was about to crack in half with the lie. "I see respect. Success."

"Fuck. You don't know me at all, asshole," the cop said. He looked at his partner. "Let's get out of here. We're wasting our time." The other cop gazed back at me for a second as if he could see right through the mask to my face sweating on the other side, my eyes shut tight, happy for once to have the plastic skull between me and the world, and then he shrugged and turned and followed his partner to the car.

I walked back inside feeling my shirt sticking to my back, so dizzy I sat down on the stairs in the TV room, which is where Benjamin found me.

"Did you see something bad?" he asked.

"I think you know," I said.

"Yes," he whispered. It was only then that I saw he was filming me, and enraged I slapped the camera out of his hand so hard it shattered on the floor.

"This isn't funny anymore."

Benjamin stared at the shattered camera. "Do you ever," he said after a while, "do you ever see anything bad happening to us?"

I looked at him. Did he or did he not know that just by asking the question he was forcing me to look, that already it was pouring in, the murmuring hiss, the pictures of what would happen to him and Henry and Molly and Lucy. I pressed my hands to my ears as if stopping sound on the outside might stop the sound inside, only to find that it increased it, the soundtrack to the future so clear it might as well have been a roar.

I was so desperate for silence it took a second to see that Benjamin was crying, and I got up and collected the bits of broken camera and brought them to him and put my arm around his shoulders saying we'd get it fixed, and if not we'd buy a new one.

"It isn't that," he said, looking at the pieces in his lap. "Did you know that Grandpa gives Henry aspirin whenever we go over there and he has a cold or a headache or something? I keep telling him not to, it's bad to give kids aspirin, but he keeps doing it, saying people have been using aspirin for hundreds of years, and I tell him kids have been dying for hundreds of years!"

I nodded, closed my eyes, saw it in my head, the risk of Reye's Syndrome, only it was Henry now, not some anonymous kid in a hospital bed, our little redhead, four years old, his little body comatose then thrashing on the sheets as his internal organs shut down one by one. I opened my eyes and shook my head to clear it.

"One time," Benjamin continued, "you asked me to watch Molly and Lucy and they both ran out into the road. But they were going in opposite directions, and I didn't know which one to get to first."

"I shouldn't have left you alone with them," I said, remembering how shaken he'd been when I came back, holding both girls by the hands as they screamed and struggled to get away. But I was no longer really in the conversation. I was somewhere else. Which of the girls was I seeing now? I wondered. She must have been seventy, slowly crossing the street, hobbling on the end of a cane, the rain so heavy there was no way that the oncoming car could see her. "Stop!" I shouted—not to Benjamin but the car.

But it was Benjamin who stopped. He waited a second. "But, see, Dad, I'm just scared, and so I'm imagining things. But you—you've got power. You can actually see what's going to happen! You could make a million dollars! Even more."

"Benjamin, you need to go . . ."

"I'm serious, Dad. With my videos, plus some newspaper articles, we could put up a website, and we could charge people . . ."

"Benjamin, get up to bed." I was frantic with his craziness. "Get in the shower, brush your teeth, put on your pajamas."

I turned to watch him go upstairs, and that's when I saw the little body huddled on the landing, pressed to the wall, shivering in his pajamas. It was Henry. As usual, he'd caught Benjamin and me talking and snuck out of bed to listen, only this time he wasn't so happy with what he'd overheard.

"Henry, what are you doing here?" I whispered, trying not to wake the girls, reaching down and putting my arms around him, feeling his head settling against my shoulder, his body limp. It was like reaching after something thin as a shadow, like trying to put my arms around an etching of a boy gouged into the wall.

"Dad, is Benjy going to die?"

"No," I said. "No, I mean . . ." I thought of saying something about how he'd die eventually, a long time from now, so long in fact that Henry wouldn't have to worry about it, but I decided to just let the sentence fade on my lips.

"Terry Fox died," Henry said, recalling the cancer-stricken runner, and the commemoration of his Marathon of Hope Henry had taken part in, along with his class, a week ago, the details of which probably shouldn't have been taught to a four-year-old, or at least not in the way they had been. "They had to cut off his leg when he was running across Canada to save sick people from cancer," Henry mumbled. "Then he died."

"Yes," I said. "He died."

"Sometimes people who are young have to have their legs cut off," Henry said, shivering in my arms as I went up the last few stairs and turned into his bedroom. "Were Terry Fox's mom and dad mad at him for dying?" he asked, and the way he held onto my shirt, both of his tiny fists grasping at the fabric, it seemed like he'd been working on the question for months, scared of the answer. "Mom would miss me if I died," he said.

"They weren't mad at him," I said. "They were sad." But this didn't seem like it offered anything better for him to think about. "They were probably happy that being sick wasn't hurting him any more," I said.

"His leg?" Henry said.

"No. Yes. Everything." I couldn't figure out what to say.

"Sometimes kids die," Henry murmured.

I lifted the blanket over him, not wanting to look at the question hidden inside what he was saying, afraid of seeing it even for a second. "You're not going to die," I whispered. It was a lie, we both knew it, but it made both of us feel better.

"Dad," he asked as I was going out, "did you see that I wasn't going to die?"

"Yes," I said. "That's what I saw. Don't be afraid, Henry. Just go to sleep."

But it was too late, the noise had awakened the girls, and since Marcy was downstairs watching TV I stepped into their room, and in a minute my eyes adjusted to the dark, and I saw they were standing in their cribs, crying and calling my name. It was always like this, one of our kids would get upset, or start to laugh, or just express neediness, and it would spread, making its way from kid to kid like a virus, and by the time we'd calmed the last one down it had come back around to the first. I took Molly out of her crib in one arm, Lucy out of hers in the other, and sat with them on the floor in the dark, feeling their hearts beating in their rib cages. It was Lucy who said it, garbled at first, but as she repeated the words I realized it wasn't just nonsense syllables, there was something there, some intelligence: *"Profert Mortem."* She lifted her head off my shoulder and recoiled from my face as if I was unfamiliar, as if she didn't recognize me. It sounded like a question, another of those words like "fuck" or "shit" she'd overheard and needed confirmed, preferably in a sentence that provided context: "Yes, that plumber who said he fixed our toilet was a real fuck," or, "Lucy, it's three in the morning and I'm not interested in taking any more of your shit."

Was she speaking Latin? *"Profert mortem?"* I said. "Is that what you're saying?"

She looked at me in fright: *"Profert mortem."* What did that mean? In her eyes was as clear an accusation as I'd ever seen. I could smell sweat on my face.

"Okay," I said. "*Profert mortem. Profert mortem* is okay."

But their hearts kept beating hard for another five minutes, and getting them back into bed was so awkward they both woke a little, and I had to stand there between the cribs running my fingers through their hair until they'd gone back to sleep.

Marcy called from downstairs. "Wally Bifford insisted you call him back. He made me promise," she said, shuddering. "What a creep." She looked at the TV, and then stayed that way, fixed to the screen. "Are the kids in bed?" she asked, still transfixed.

"Yes," I said. I could see her crumbling in front of me, as if it was more than light coming from the television, as if it was something hotter, and she was defenseless against it. "Do you know what *profert mortem* means?"

She pulled over her laptop and typed it into Google. "He/she/it brings forth death," she said. "That's morbid." I looked at her remembering how Lucy had glared at me in the dark, as if I was the thing that had woken her, the nightmare man himself, come into the room to remind her that by bringing her and her siblings into the world he had in some way also ensured their deaths, and I wanted to run back into her room and say, "Hey, your mother *profert mortem,* too," but I just scratched my head and said, "I guess I'll go call Wally."

"Things go okay with the police?"

"Yeah," I said. "Routine stuff." But Marcy had already turned up the volume.

It wasn't until I picked up the phone and turned to the mirror over the fireplace that I realized I was still wearing the mask, that I'd been wearing it all along, ever since the cop asked me to put it on—worn it during my conversation with Benjamin, while I'd consoled Henry and the girls, and talked to Marcy—and none of them had noticed. Why hadn't Henry said something? Why hadn't Molly and Lucy, usually so sensitive to that, screamed when they saw me? I looked closer at my reflection, tilting my head this way and that, looking for the line where the mask ended and my skin began, feeling around for it, reaching for the strap that was no longer there, and finally looking into the mirror itself as if the only way to get it off would be to reach in there and tear it away. I was about to tell myself to stop being silly and just remove it when the phone rang.

"Hey, great that I got you, buddy," Wally said. "Great, great. Listen, I don't want to take up much of your time, I know it's after hours and all that, but I'm thinking of dumping some stock tomorrow, you know, with Bart's death and the whole reorg and all, and I was wondering whether you—I know this sounds crazy, so just indulge me, okay—whether you had any optics on that? I mean, should I wait another day? Is there going to be some kind of rebound?" He waited. I closed my eyes, trying to picture some clichéd image of a price ticker on the New York Stock Exchange. When Wally spoke next he was angry. "Listen, I know you haven't gotten another job. You gotta be getting desperate. I could hire you back right now, right here, just say the word."

And then I knew what I had to say, what I had to do. I accepted the mask, let it merge with my face, and turned toward the terrible vision, following it to the horizon and beyond, down into that cratered landscape where we were all working together, skeleton after skeleton after skeleton, me and my brothers dancing along across meadows and waterfronts and mountaintops herding the men and women and children onto scaffolds, into ovens and cages and the mouths of lions, off cliffs into raging seas. I looked around and knew what I had to do, rising with my terrible power, lifting the receiver with my bone fingers to the hole in the side of my skull, gazing with my empty eye sockets into Wally's future to tell him exactly how it would be. "Wally," I said, the sound hollow in my throat, the letters and syllables clattering off my teeth, "you have more important things to worry about, especially that half bottle of scotch you drink every . . ."

"Yeah, yeah, sure," Wally said. "That's what my doctor says. The long-term effect of booze and all that. But I'm thinking in the short term here," he continued, "and in the short term I need to know if I should buy or sell."

From the corner of my eye I could see one of the skeletons, his body appearing and disappearing behind a cloud of black smoke rising from the furnaces, concealing a child who looked a lot like him—the same bone structure—behind a small boulder, reaching into his hip socket and pulling out a chocolate bar and handing it over, lifting his cell phone to his ear and yelling into it to make himself heard above the booming of artillery and the screams of the dying, "Yes, yes, she's with me. No everything's fine. Yes, I'm planning to sit down with her and do some homework after dinner." The skeleton saw me staring and glared back, daring me to say a word.

"I'm going to save you, Wally," I finally said into the phone.

"How much?" he asked. "How much are you going to save me? What are we talking in terms of? A grand, a hundred grand, a million—what?"

"I'm going to save all of us," I continued. I was in the movie now, one step ahead of the present, moving in that stiff way skeletons do along the landscape of death, and I looked back at that other skeleton, now crouching by the boulder with a math textbook and a pencil in his hands and explaining long division to the little girl, and I decided I was going to do the same, that knowing the future was enough to change it, that Wally and me and my wife and children and all of us were going to live forever. "My eyes can see to the end of time," I said to Wally, "and it's going to be okay."

"Well, let's not get ahead of ourselves, okay buddy?" he replied. "You gotta leave some time for the present, you know what I'm saying? So for now there's just one question: Do we go with the short term on this stock, or dig in for the big payoff at the end?"

Paul Verlaine

A Woman and Her Cat

She was playing with her little cat
—a female, black. From where I sat

in the shadows, it was entrancing,
watching the dancing

bat-bat back and forth
of their white hand-paws, by the hearth.

One of them had hidden away
—wicked thing!—inside her kitty-

mittens, the murderous
curved agates of her claws,

sleek and slicing as razors.
The other, too, was like so much sugar,

and only seemed to have withdrawn
her own stinging talons.

The Devil—never far away—
would not go cheated of his daily pay:

later, in the bedroom,
where it was heavier, the gloom,

with her every laugh, light
and bell-like in the night

but also sure and sonorous,
were four bright points of phosphorus.

*— Translated from the French[1] of Paul Verlaine
by Diane Furtney*

---

[1] See "Translation Notes," *"Femme et chatte"* on page 195 for the original French version.

Teresa Milbrodt

The Passion of Jude

Patron saint of lost causes, desperate situations, and high school reunions,
sits at the bar nursing a club soda as middle-aged men drink cheap beer
and middle-aged women cake on makeup, covering years of sun worship.
Half the class flings grandkid photos, the other half feels impossibly old.

Jude watches singles clutch drinks like life preservers. They wonder why
they broke up with the last boy or girlfriend, should have waited a month,
come here resembling happiness. They are not accustomed to flying solo,
need an arm to clutch, an anchor for the evening. Jude smooths his violet robe.

The biology and algebra teachers—retired and seventy-something—crash
the gala, home from Maui. They have a condo time-share and tanned
wrinkles, discuss whale watching with former students still lost in mazes
of children, nine-to-five jobs, eyes glued to stock market pensions.

Jude listens to half-crocked victims of broken marriages, song-and-dance
divorce routines complete with custody battles and legal fees. He nods sympathy.
Halo hazed with cigarette smoke and defeat: things should have been better. Jude
gives advice: go out for cheeseburgers, milkshakes; have a glass of wine at home.

You are, he says, blessedly normal.

Peter Austin

Twenty Years On

Each Jack within the group had found his Jill,
Successfully, you guessed from their deportment,
Even the oddest match in the assortment—
A schoolmarm so punctilious, so chill
You knew she'd never warmed a boyfriend's bed
And a roué who'd fertilized more ova
(At least by his account) than Casanova
And swore that he'd have made Our Lady spread.

Twenty years on, you look around and see
A mess of separations, shaky truces
(Not for the parents' sake but Jane's or Bruce's)
And, circumnavigating the debris,
Who but the oddest matchup, hand in hand,
Acting as if they lived in Neverland.

FICTION

Maxine Rosaler
The Uncle

I met Isaac's uncle only once. I showed up at his store on Orchard Street late one afternoon in July with the hope of catching Isaac there but when I arrived his uncle told me Isaac was "out collecting." I asked if it would be all right for me to wait, and he nodded toward a carton in the back that was piled high with blue jeans wrapped in cellophane.

"It's all right. Sit. They don't bite," he said with a sudden grin. And that was the last thing he said to me. He sat staring out into the street as if he were waiting for something, though from the sad look on his sad face it didn't seem to matter to him whether or not what he was waiting for would ever come. He didn't speak. He seemed to be as comfortable with silence as he was with waiting and after a while I gave up trying to strike up a conversation with him, although it made me extremely uneasy to be there, saying nothing, just waiting. He sat on that broken-down chair as though it were a throne—his back perfectly straight, his arms folded across his chest, commanding the air.

Under the black web of his beard and the imposing bulk of his belly I was surprised to see how much he resembled Isaac. He had the same narrow wrists and the same long fingers—sensitive fingers, meant for the delicate work of breaking hearts, not the sort to be spending a lifetime testing fabrics and counting money. In almost every respect he seemed to be a modified version of Isaac—blown up here, stretched out and sagging there, but basically the same, except around the mouth, which was stretched tightly across his teeth like an elastic band. Isaac had lips like a silent screen star's. I loved those lips.

When Isaac burrowed his way into the store an hour later he didn't notice me. He headed straight for his uncle, who listened to his account of the day's business. After Isaac had finished, his uncle allowed several seconds of silence to penetrate the air and then he said slowly in his heavy European accent: "The money. It stays in their pockets. It gets warm. They think it's theirs."

Isaac and I had worked together as reporters for a chain of community newspapers in Brooklyn. The first time I saw him he was wearing a plaid shirt and a white tie. I remember thinking how the outfit suited him, but later on that day I decided that it didn't really suit him at all. It was his first day on the job, and Barry, the editor, introduced us saying: "Isaac will be covering the Flatbush beat. He lives there, poor kid. Why don't you take him down to Passetti's and show him the ropes?"

At Passetti's, long before the coffee arrived, Isaac confessed to me that he didn't really live in Flatbush. He was from there, but he didn't live there anymore. He had only told Barry that so he could get the job. He lived in a studio apartment in the West Village.

He was just out of college and five years younger than I and that seemed to be good enough reasons to forgo the possibility of romance, but when four weeks later I was offered a job on another paper the thought of never seeing him again left me with a sick feeling in the pit of my stomach. He was there that Friday when I went to pick up my last paycheck, and without thinking about it I asked him for his number. He wrote it down in the reporter's notebook that he kept in the breast pocket of his jacket, and after tearing out the page and giving it to me he asked me to give him mine.

I don't remember who called whom for our first date, but I remember every other detail of that evening. It was a freakishly warm night around Thanksgiving and there was a summer-like heaviness in the air that had absorbed all the sounds and blended everything—the horns honking, the car wheels sweeping across the pavement, the children playing in the street—into one slightly muffled, faraway din.

We met at his apartment on West Thirteenth Street. Isaac sat chastely on the narrow studio bed with its boy's bedspread—the kind that is brown with an ugly plaid—and he told me stories about his adventures as a cub reporter. As I sat across from him in his big creaky leather chair I kept on wanting to go over to him and put my arms around his neck and say: "Why are you so sad, baby?"

We went to an Indian restaurant on East Sixth Street. A warm breeze was blowing and the streets of the East Village were quieter than usual. It was as though everything had slowed down to make way for the dramatic change in the weather. On the sidewalks of Saint Mark's Place the peddlers displayed secondhand clothes and books on moldy shower curtains and torn pieces of brightly colored velvet, and in front of the Astor Place subway station a happy crowd of people gathered around a six-piece band that was playing "Begin the Beguine." We saw a teenage boy whose shaven head was covered with a tattoo that said FUCK EVERYTHING leading a pretty green-haired girl down Eighth Street by a metal chain. Isaac was wearing his plaid shirt and white tie and I was wearing a red dress and he kept on telling me how beautiful I was.

We walked all over the Village, in circles it seemed, and finally when the strap of my left shoe broke off at the ankle I said that it was late and that I'd better be getting home. He walked me to a bus stop. When we saw the bus coming up Third Avenue we looked at each other and didn't say anything. The bus pulled up to the curb and after the last of the passengers had gotten on and it was my turn to board Isaac took hold of my elbow and asked me if I'd like to come back to his place for a game of Parcheesi.

Soon we were back in his barren apartment and he was lifting a finger to his lips in a plea for silence and he was padding his way down the hall to turn off the overhead light and he was padding his way back and draping a red shirt over the shade of the desk lamp that stood by his bed. He undressed me slowly in the red darkness, a look of astonishment shining across his face.

Three weeks passed before I saw Isaac again. For some reason I knew I couldn't expect to hear from him, but after calling his number day after day after day and not reaching him, I felt that I was going to go mad. I kept on telling myself that we had spent only one night together, but I couldn't stop replaying every moment of that night; I couldn't stop remembering what it had felt like to be with him in his narrow little bed. Finally I got the idea of calling Barry and on some pretext inquiring about Isaac. When Barry told me Isaac had quit the paper, I felt even more confused.

"But I thought he was doing so well. He was so happy," I said.

"Yeah. It threw me for a loop too." I could see him shrugging through the phone. "He was going to take over my job. Weinstein made me assistant publisher and I recommended Isaac for the job. I thought he was going to fall down on his fucking knees and kiss my fucking feet, he was so grateful. Then he calls and tells me he can't take it. That he has to go work at his uncle's store on Orchard Street. He sounded like death warmed over and started apologizing to me like he let me down in some really big way."

"Did he give you a number?" I asked.

"Yeah. Let me see—yeah here it is. He wanted me to let him know if any leads came in on the MTA story he was working on. He asked me if it would be all right if he finished it, even though he wasn't working here anymore."

I had to dial the number three times before I got it right. My first try I got a police precinct in Harlem. The second time there was a man cursing me out in Chinese. Finally, it was Isaac, sounding frighteningly unlike himself, singing into the phone, "B&G Clothing."

"Isaac?" I said. It was a full three seconds before he responded. But then there was that same eerily cheerful lilt to his voice. "Oh hi, Lisa," he said.

"Isaac, I was so worried."

"What's to be worried about?" he asked, still with the same false cheer.

"I didn't know what happened to you," I explained. "At first I thought God-knows-what. Then I thought, maybe it was me. Maybe it was something with me."

"Oh no, Lisa," he said. "Why would you ever think that?"

"Isaac, would you like to see me?"

"Yes," he said. His sincerity engulfed me. "Of course I want to see you."

We arranged to meet at a small Spanish restaurant in his neighborhood. It was a quiet, friendly place, with only a few tables occupied and everyone smiled at us when we came in. Our waiter, a grandfatherly man who walked with a slight limp, brought us two glasses of red wine, compliments of the house.

Isaac dipped his pinky into his glass and gently rubbed my lips. "It's nice like this," he whispered as he leaned over to kiss me, the sweet taste of the wine blending with the sweet smoky taste of his mouth.

When we got back to his apartment Isaac asked me if I'd like to take a bubble bath with him. In his enthusiasm he ended up dumping the contents of the entire bottle into the tub. He soaped up his hands and let them glide slowly up and down my back, under my arms and across my chest.

"You're too good to me, Lisa," he said as he kissed me on the back of the neck. "I don't deserve this." I wanted to believe he was kidding, but I knew he wasn't.

Isaac didn't think he deserved to be happy. He would always greet the simplest pleasure, the smallest kindness, with an appreciation bordering on wonderment. It was as though he were a refugee from a totalitarian state where things like holding hands in public and eating breakfast in bed were not permitted, where having a girlfriend who loved you was against the law.

As it turned out I was doing all the calling. But I didn't let that bother me. Isaac was always so happy to hear from me, so happy just to be with me. He would always greet me with the same sweet surprised, "Hello, Lisa, how are you?" when I called, and when we were together he would always thank me just for being with him, and when we made love he would always undress me with the same delicate care and attention; yet I knew from the start that I was losing him, or rather, the possibility of ever having him. He was always tired and two or three hours into the evening he would fall asleep, usually on top of me. I would stay crushed under the weight of his body until it was no longer possible for me to breathe. Sometimes he would talk in his sleep. It was usually just one or two words and it was always about the business. The longest sentence I ever heard him say in his sleep was: "The Levis'll be here tomorrow."

He would wake up at 4:59, a minute before the alarm was set to go off, then he'd slip out of my arms carefully, so as not to wake me, and go about his morning rituals, marking each task with a deep sigh. He would sigh when he brushed his teeth; he would sigh when he sat at his desk sipping a cup of black coffee, and, standing at the window, smoking the first cigarette of the day, he would sigh again. Then he would pace up and down the narrow room—from the apartment's one window to the opposite wall that held his Abbott and Costello poster and back again—all the time muttering under his breath, "Shit. Shit. Shit."

Several times after Isaac started working at his uncle's store I told him I wanted to visit him there, but whenever I suggested it, he would either change the subject or come up with an excuse. There was a big shipment of blue jeans coming in that day. There was a customer he had to see. They were in the middle of doing inventory. Once when he couldn't come up with an excuse right away he blurted out, "But how would I introduce you? Who could I say you were?"

It was morning and we were sitting in a coffee shop in the East Village eating breakfast and Isaac started shredding his napkin and rolling the pieces into little white balls. "Your girlfriend," I responded. "That's what I am. Isn't it?" He was squirming in his seat, swaying nervously from side to side like a blind man. But I pressed on. "Isaac, isn't that what I am? Aren't I your girlfriend and aren't you my boyfriend? Aren't we boyfriend and girlfriend?" I held my breath and waited for him to answer.

"He wouldn't understand," Isaac answered finally.

Then he went on to tell me about his uncle. How every day after yeshiva, when the other boys were hiding their yarmulkes away in their schoolbags and going to play stick ball in the streets, he would grab his candy bar and baseball bat and rush to take the F train to go to Orchard Street to stand guard over the underwear and jeans. He worked there throughout college too—every day of the week but Saturday, when he would drag three heavy cardboard ledgers home and spend the morning and most of the afternoon poring over the thinly lined pages, running the columns of figures through the adding machine his uncle had given him for his bar mitzvah. The Uncle (that's how Isaac always referred to him) had always been the center of his universe. Since he was a boy, Isaac had loved him, more than he would ever dare to love himself.

The Uncle became an invisible presence in our lives. Isaac would talk about him all the time and always with such passion that everything outside of the world of Orchard Street—that site of the immigrant's struggles and triumphs—would seem unreal and insignificant, including me.

Sometimes he would make up songs for his uncle and he would sing them to me. Or he would buy little presents for him: a pair of suspenders, a hat, an engraved bowling ball. Once, out of the blue he said to me, "Do you know why I get up at five every morning to go to Orchard Street to wholesale? The Uncle. I can't believe how much I love that man!"

The image of the uncle began to loom large in my life as well. He would appear with remarkable clarity in my dreams: We were always great friends, we laughed a lot together, told each other jokes, once we shared a pot roast sandwich and a can of celery soda on a giant field of bright blue denim grass.

Isaac never told me so exactly, but from the start I knew that I couldn't expect to see him more than once a week—on Saturday, the only day he didn't have to labor at his uncle's store. Sometimes I wouldn't bother to call. I would just show up at his door. Of course, I always held on to the hope that all that would change once Isaac grew more accustomed to me, or, rather, the idea of me.

New Year's Eve fell on a Wednesday that year. I assumed we would spend it together, but when I suggested it to Isaac, he looked surprised, almost disoriented. We were standing in front of the IRT subway station. My arms were wrapped around his waist, my face was buried in his chest and I was breathing in the familiar scent of Irish Spring soap. I could feel his body stiffen slightly and I let go and started to move away from him. But then Isaac put his hands on my shoulders and looked into my eyes. "I'd love to spend New Year's with you, Lisa," he said. "We'll paint the town."

Isaac had decorated his small apartment with balloons and streamers. He had slicked his hair back with something wet and sticky that smelled like bubble gum. I had gotten dressed up in a black velvet dress and high heels and Isaac stood leaning against the wall gaping at me in silence. I started to laugh and I went over to him and put my arms around his neck and kissed him.

"You look so serious, baby," I said and I kissed him again. He started tugging at the collar of my dress, clumsily, like a kid who didn't know the first thing about being with a girl. I thought he was going to rip it and although I felt inclined to let him tear the fucking thing off, I guided his fingers to the zipper in the back.

He smiled at me then, that sly smile of his, and lifted his eyebrows slightly and said politely, "May I?" He unzipped me with special care and slipped the dress over my head. "Wait right here, don't go away," he said as he went and lay the dress over the back of his creaky leather chair. We made love standing up against the wall, right there in the hall. Afterward Isaac found a fifty-cent stamp crumpled up in his bottom desk drawer and he pasted it on the spot. He said we would make love in every square foot of the apartment and that before the year was out it would have enough postage on it to be mailed to Australia.

We spent the rest of the evening drinking champagne and dancing with the people at the New Year's Eve party on Channel 4. We never gave any thought to going out and at eleven we ordered Chinese takeout from the all-night place down the block. Isaac gave me a pair of his pajamas to wear and we laid his plaid bedspread out on the floor and had a picnic, all the while raving about the fine cuisine and the marvelous decor.

Just before he drifted off to sleep, a little past midnight, Isaac whispered in my ear, "This is going to be my best year ever." And then, so softly that I thought I might be imagining it, he added, "Because of you, you, you."

Isaac arose before dawn the next morning, out of habit, I suppose. I woke up with him and told him that I wanted to go to the Lower East Side for breakfast. We held hands and walked through the deserted streets in silence. I had never before seen the city at dawn. The streetlights were still shining and the moon was still hanging in a dusty sky. Only the coo of a pigeon standing on the windowsill of an abandoned building disrupted the impenetrable quiet.

It was a very cold day and the streets were empty. New York City looked like a ghost town. We walked through the Village, past the scattered remains of the previous night's celebrations. A bunch of half-deflated balloons floated past us as we crossed Grand Street. I told Isaac that my parents used to take me here when I was a little girl. Even then this part of the city held an enchantment for me. But today there were no old Jewish merchants standing glumly in doorways, their arms folded across their chests. There were no bins upon bins of dried fruits and nuts or endless barrels of pickles. There was no profusion of shirts and dresses hanging from metal racks standing crookedly on cracked sidewalks. Today all the storefronts were covered up with metal gates and the streets were empty.

Isaac led me to a restaurant that had huge hunks of sponge cake and pieces of pie displayed on cardboard in a dirty glass window. A woman wearing a blue-and-gray-flowered kerchief served us poached eggs and creamed spinach in efficient silence. Sitting there with Isaac at this gray Formica table in this ancient restaurant in this timeless part of the city, I felt like a tourist and this made me uncomfortable, for I knew that Isaac was no tourist here. When I told him this he looked at me and said, "I got middle-aged and died here."

"What a thing to say, Isaac," I said.

"Just kidding," he said.

After breakfast he asked me if I would like to visit his uncle's store. It was covered, like all the stores up and down the street, with heavy metal gates. Across the street a wooden sign written in Hebrew creaked in the wind. Isaac took a set of keys out of his pocket and one by one proceeded to unlock the heavy bolts that held the gates together. He deftly accommodated himself to the idiosyncrasies of each lock, jiggling one here, tugging at another there. He rolled the gates open. The crash of metal against metal interrupted the still quiet of the cold morning.

We walked into a room that was crowded with cartons of blue jeans. Near the door was a glass counter patched over in several places with pieces of duct tape which were dirty and curling up around the edges. Next to it, in an even greater state of disrepair, was an old armchair. One of its arms was worn down beyond the stuffing to the bare wood and under its sagging seat a piece of coiled metal popped out like the naked neck of a headless, upside down Jack-in-the box. Off to the right a wall had been knocked down and there were pieces of plaster and brick lying in a heap on the floor. Isaac explained that his uncle had recently bought the building next door. He led me through the opening in the wall and told me about the plans his uncle had for expanding the business.

"We're going to get the material from Korea and do the manufacturing in China." Isaac picked a rubber band off the floor and started twisting it tightly around his fingers.

"But, I thought—" I paused, for I wanted to choose my words carefully. I had never asked Isaac why he had quit the paper to go to work for his uncle on Orchard Street, or why he never called me, or why he was always so difficult to reach. I knew it would be pointless to do so. But I knew this was important. Isaac's whole future—*our* future—depended on it.

Finally I said, "But I thought all this was temporary."

Isaac pulled the rubber band more tightly around his fingers. The tips of his pinkies and thumbs turned a reddish purple.

"Everyone one else was killed," he said finally. "There's nobody else but me."

He started standing me up. I didn't see it as a pattern at first. Every time it happened it was such a shock, such a hurt. It did no good to ask him what was wrong; his only explanation was that he was "out of control." Phrases like that started creeping with increasing regularity into his conversation.

One night in the middle of July, I decided that I couldn't take it anymore. Isaac had said he would call for me at eight and by eight-thirty I knew he wouldn't be showing up. I kept on phoning him at ten-minute intervals, although I knew he wouldn't answer the phone even if he was there. Isaac often didn't answer his phone. I could see him, sitting in his chair, letting it ring over and over again. It never seemed to bother him how many times the phone rang or the loudness of the ring or the fact that there was someone on the other end who wanted desperately to speak to him.

I had just stupidly washed the white rug in my living room with ammonia and Clorox—a lethal combination to begin with and one that was made even more lethal by the hot humid air that crawled in through the window. There was no escaping the fumes or the tiny pieces of invisible dust that tickled my throat all night long. I called in sick at work the next day and stayed balanced on the thought that I would go down to Orchard Street at five and tell Isaac that I couldn't see him anymore. But when I saw him there with his uncle, looking so humble and defeated, I knew I wouldn't be able to go through with it. The frustration I'd felt that night with the fumes and the heat and the dust, and all the other nights of not hearing from him and not knowing why vanished in his presence. All I could feel was this overwhelming love. My love for Isaac made me powerless.

Later on that evening he told me he loved me for the first and only time. We were sitting in a red plastic booth in a bar in Chinatown not far from his uncle's store and a crowd of off-duty policemen had just come in to watch a baseball game on the television that hung suspended in the air above two rows of dusty glasses. I was trying to tell him how much his disappearances upset me.

"Hit me. Go on. Hit me," he said and he reached out and rolled my fingers into a fist and bounced the fist against his chin. "I deserve it." Then he uncapped the fountain pen he'd taken from its place next to the reporter's notebook he still carried in the breast pocket of his jacket and smoothed his napkin out on the table. On it he drew a rebus containing an eye with long curly lashes, a big heart and a U. The paper napkin was too porous for the ink of a fountain pen and tiny beads of ink, like tiny black pearls, had formed wherever his hand had faltered.

I asked him if he would like to go away with me somewhere and we made plans to take a trip to Atlantic City the following weekend. I knew that Isaac had never gone away with a woman before and that made the prospect all the more exciting for me to contemplate. But I didn't hear from him all that following week. By that time I had instituted a policy of holding off calling him for as long as I could bear it and I let another week pass before I called. I knew something was wrong as soon as he answered the phone. When I asked him how he was he said in a voice that was barely audible, "Not good."

And when I asked him what was wrong he didn't say anything. I asked him again. "My uncle, my uncle," he began. "My uncle, my uncle . . ." and then he hung up the phone.

The funeral was in an area of Brooklyn Isaac used to refer to as Torah Town. It was an unbearably hot day. The heat seemed to rise from the sidewalk in curly white waves. Despite the heat, the women all wore long skirts and wigs and heavy shoes and the men were dressed in black suits and black hats. They had beards and sidelocks they tucked behind their ears. The funeral parlor was crowded with people who spoke in whispers to each other. No one was speaking to Isaac when I walked into the room. He sat in the corner near the coffin with his mother. She was a small, pretty woman with blond hair. She was much younger than I had expected her to be and she smiled at me sweetly when I gave her my hand. I didn't dare touch Isaac. He looked dangerously untouchable, sternly fragile.

After the rabbi had recited Psalm 23, Isaac walked up to the podium to deliver the eulogy. He told the story of his uncle. How he had managed to keep himself and his sister alive during the three years they had spent in a concentration camp, how he had come to this country with nothing and had built a business—B&G—the largest wholesale clothing store on the Lower East Side. How after Isaac's father had died suddenly he had looked after his sister and her young family. He described how in some ways his uncle was like a kid—he loved watching bowling on TV, he loved his pot roast sandwiches and celery soda. And he loved his business. It had been like a child to him. He had brought it into the world and raised it into something he could be proud of. This was his legacy. Here Isaac paused and turned to the coffin and pledged he would do his best to take over where his uncle had left off, to follow through on the plans he had made for the store before he died.

I looked for Isaac outside the chapel but I couldn't find him for several minutes. He was just about to get into a limousine when I spotted him finally. I ran over and grabbed hold of him with all my might. His arms hung lifelessly at his side and his cheek recoiled slightly from the touch of my lips.

On my way past the parking lot a big, fatherly looking man who introduced himself as Ben Levine asked me if I needed a ride to the cemetery. As I sank into the soft blue leather of the front seat of his Cadillac I felt a small wave of relief, like someone was going to take care of me.

"It's hot," he said to me in a heavy Eastern European accent. He took a handkerchief out of his shirt pocket and wiped the sweat from his forehead, took off his jacket and laid it carefully across the back seat. Then he unlatched a pair of diamond cuff links and rolled up the sleeves of his shirt. He pressed a pearl white button on the dashboard.

"It will be cool in a second," he said to me. "The air conditioner in this car works like a dream." A gust of lukewarm air swept across my face and a soft and steady purring filled the car.

It wasn't until after we were on the Brooklyn Queens Expressway headed for the cemetery that I noticed the series of blue-black numbers tattooed on his forearm just above the wrist. Whenever I'm confronted with that image I always return to my original perception of it. Max the Tailor, who had a shop in Oceanside, where I grew up, had those numbers on his arm and when I was a little girl I asked my mother about them. She told me about the cattle cars and the lampshades and the pillows and the soap, and the showers that weren't really showers. Some time after that Max gave me an old mannequin of his to play with. She was covered with torn brown canvas and she emanated a stale, musty odor. I named her Matilda and dressed her in an old dress of my mother's. I tried to play with her, but I couldn't play with her. I couldn't play with any of my other toys either, with her standing there in my room with her eyeless eyes, her armless, legless, faceless torso. One night I woke up screaming from a dream about faceless men sticking pins in my eyes and the next day when I came home from school Matilda was gone. But I didn't forget her for a long time afterward.

Mr. Levine and I drove along in silence near the front row of cars that made up the funeral procession. From the rear view mirror I could see cars with their headlights on moving slowly through the summer heat. The cars to the left of us and the cars to the right of us whizzed past, distant and removed from the business of Isaac's uncle's death. I had no idea what Mr. Levine was thinking about but it comforted me to imagine that we were sharing a different piece of the same enormous grief.

Back at Isaac's mother's house in Flatbush the merchants of the Lower East Side gathered to pay their respects. Isaac sat on the sofa talking to a man with a beard who was dressed in a long black coat. His mother sat on a cardboard box imprinted with the pattern of wood. Her hands were folded in her lap and she spoke softly, every now and then bringing a hand to her cheek and turning her head from side to side, her eyes never leaving Isaac.

I sat down beside her and she extended her hand to me.

"Isaac didn't tell me he had such a pretty friend," she said with a weak smile. "What? You know him from college?"

"We were reporters together," I told her.

"On the school paper?"

"No. On the paper in Brooklyn."

"In Brooklyn?" She sounded confused. I realized that the job must have been a secret, just as I had been a secret. I looked at her. At her blond hair and her fair skin and her heavy eyes. Her mouth was very thin and it was cast in a strained smile. I hated her for not even thinking that her son might have a girlfriend. Why should Isaac suffer, why should I suffer, just because she had suffered?

"I'm very sorry," I said. "I know your brother was a remarkable man. Isaac loved him very much."

She looked at me and shook her head and said, "Too much. Too much."

I called Isaac every day for a week after the funeral. After closing up the store he would go home to his mother's and I would call him there in the evenings. She would answer the phone. We developed a rapport based on our mutual concern for

Isaac. After asking how she was getting on, a matter of little consequence as far as she was concerned, I would ask about Isaac.

"Not good," she would respond with a sigh. "He doesn't eat. He plays with his food, but he doesn't eat it. I make all his favorites. I know he doesn't want to hurt my feelings. He says, 'I'm sorry, I know it's delicious but I'm not hungry. Maybe tomorrow. Save it for me tomorrow.' And then he goes downstairs to Sol's room. It's not good."

Whenever Isaac came to the phone he would greet me with a falsely cheerful hello and when I asked him how he was he would say, "Fine." I told him I missed him. That I wanted to be with him.

"Don't you think it would make you feel better if you saw me? I just want to make you feel better," I would say, careful not to push too hard. Usually he wouldn't respond at all, but if I persisted long enough sometimes he would abandon the facade and in a voice filled with despair he would tell me that there was so much to do, that there was never enough time. As it turned out his uncle had left everything to him. Isaac had been the sole heir ever since he was thirteen years old.

When he went back to stay in his apartment I would call him there, but he never answered the phone. He was there. I knew he was there. I could see him sitting in his creaky leather chair, letting the phone ring. I would try him at the store—but he was always too busy to speak. I resorted to writing notes. At first I would just say that I missed him, that I wanted to see him. When that didn't work I started looking for excuses. I had left a little gold bracelet at his apartment. Or there was a book I had lent him that I needed. Once I just sent him a postcard with a big question mark written on it. But nothing worked and eventually I gave up. What else could I do?

Months went by and then one day I was in his neighborhood and on my way home I passed his block. It was slightly out of my way but I decided to make the detour—as a kind of experiment, I told myself, to see how I would feel. I hadn't dared walk anywhere near his street for months. I would often try to avoid the neighborhood entirely, and passing it now my heart felt an ache so strong I had trouble catching my breath and I said out loud to myself, "Idiot, what are you doing?"

It was a bright cold day in the middle of November—just cold enough to cover the puddles that had collected at the curbs and on the sidewalks with thin layers of ice. I was afraid to look up, so I directed myself to the task of inspecting what was in the puddles. They were like little glass museums of the recent past that had made relics of the street's paraphernalia.

Whatever had passed their way had been frozen by the ice and now lay displayed under their fragile windowpanes. In one puddle was trapped a wool mitten, three pennies and a broken comb. Another held a bottle cap and a few of the last bright leaves of autumn.

At first I thought he was a mirage. In all the time that had passed since I had last seen Isaac the clearest image of him had never been more than a blink away from my mind's eye. He was standing under the awning of his apartment building, leaning against the rail, smoking a cigarette, talking to the doorman. He was wearing an olive green jacket and he kept on adjusting his hat—a brown tweed cap.

My first impulse was to avoid him, and I crossed the street, but I didn't even get as far as the corner before I realized it was useless.

He didn't exhibit one bit of surprise at seeing me. I didn't make any motion to approach him and he didn't approach me either. When I asked him how he was he said he was fine, just fine. He was wholesaling. "I buy low and sell high," he said. "But how are *you?*" I asked again. "How am I? Ask why, why don't you?" he replied. "Okay then, Isaac. *Why* are you?" I asked. It was a familiar routine of his. And with a comedian's timing he answered, "For no good reason."

We went to a fancy new restaurant that had recently opened up in the neighborhood. He ordered the most expensive thing on the menu. When the check came he took out a thick pile of cash which was folded in half and he peeled off six twenties, one at a time, licking his fingers before touching each wrinkled bill.

He told me that he had a new car and he offered to drive me home. His car had that new car smell. The seats were covered in cushioned leather and the dashboard was covered in cushioned leather as well. When we got to my door I asked him if he wanted to come up.

We made love on the couch. He didn't undress me and he didn't seem to have any interest in me undressing myself either and when it was over he fell asleep on top of me. I dimmed the lights and watched him sleep. He hugged the pillow tightly against his cheek. He looked like the same sweet Isaac I had once known. Around two in the morning he started muttering something in his sleep. I couldn't make it out at first, but I could tell he was mumbling the same word, over and over again. Just as I was finally drifting off to sleep, my head on his chest and my legs locked into his, he woke me with his sleep talk. This time what he was saying was so clear that I was sure he would wake himself up. Dead. He kept on saying it over and over again. Dead. Dead. Dead.

It was still dark out; there wasn't even a trace of dawn in the sky when Isaac disentangled his legs from mine and climbed out of bed to start the day. I got up to make him coffee and I went into the living room to bring it to him. He had just finished lacing up his shoes, and looking up, he seemed flustered to see me there. "I'll make you a cup of coffee before you go, Isaac," I said to him. The apartment was so cold I was shaking and I walked over to him and wrapped my arms around his waist.

He pulled away from me and rushed to put on his hat and coat. "No, don't bother," he said as he unlocked the door. He was almost shouting. "I'll get it on the outside. I'll pay for it on the outside. I can pay." And he was gone.

I locked the door behind him and sat down on the couch. I noticed that there was a sock tucked under the rug and another one crumpled up on the cocktail table. When I reached down to pick them up I noticed they were Isaac's socks. They were the black Orlon socks he would get by the dozen from Milty the Sock Wizard on Ludlow Street. They were ribbed and had a squiggle running down each side. He'd gotten a dozen for each of us last spring—mine were black ribbed too, but without the squiggle. He must have gotten them confused.

Once before the uncle died I'd woken up at Isaac's apartment with a bad cold and I stayed in his bed when he went off to work that day. I slept away most of the morning and in the afternoon I watched old movies on TV. He had done a wash the night before and the fresh laundry was piled high on his desk. I picked up a bunch of it and pressed it to my face. I folded the shirts and underwear and towels and rolled the socks into neat little balls.

When he came home later on that evening he was surprised to see me. From the weary look on his face it seemed that it must have been a hard day for him. But it wasn't long before he was joking around with me, asking me what was for dinner, ordering me to go fetch his slippers. I complained about the housework and how the kids hadn't stopped fighting all day. He promised to get me a maid and to send the kids away to boarding school. We joked around like that for a while but when he saw the neatly folded pile of laundry in the corner he stopped joking. He held me tightly and kissed me and said he was happy I was there. Then he proceeded to juggle the socks in the air. First one, then two, then three, then he had four flying in the air at once. They swirled around so fast that I couldn't distinguish one from the other. They blended together into a blurred parabola of blue, black and white above his head.

That was the only time Isaac and I had ever spent two days together in a row and I thought of it fondly now.

Kyle Potvin

To My Children Reading My Poetry after I'm Gone

If you are anything like me, you'll look
for clues about your mom inside this book.
You'll read each poem that I wrote and cry.
Please don't. You need to know it's such a lie.
That year when I was sick and lost my hair,
I brought a cactus home: a prickly pear?
I think I only used that for the rhyme.
(That's why I made up stuff from time to time!)
That hulking boat that craved the sea? It sank.
And graduation night—I *never* drank.
Some parts are real: I rocked you in my arms,
ate gyros, frites; my mother wore gold charms.
But poets play with words, ignore the truth,
"manipulate" as Plath once said. A ruth-
less cutting, blending, marking up—that's art.
Dears, best to trust what's written in your heart.

Len Krisak

Trees in November

      Like rakes turned upside down
      Against the autumn sky,
      They fan their tines,
      Where sparse and brown
      Leaves struggle in the splines
      Before they fall and die.

Susan McLean

Short-Timer

What do you read when you know that you're dying?
"Everyone's dying," Rhina said.
But after the flurry of grief and denying,
what do you read? When you know that you're dying,
Time's too ironic, the news not worth buying.
"What happens next?" doesn't interest the dead.
What do you read when you *know* that you're dying?
"Everyone's dying," Rhina said.

ABLE MUSE WRITE PRIZE FOR FICTION, 2014 ▪ WINNER

J. Preston Witt

Lesson One

After our worksheets in Greek and Latin root-words, Father announced that Brandon and I would begin training as lifeguards. That got us excited. We always passed by the public pool on the way into town. Seated up high with their sunglasses and red swimsuits, the lifeguards looked strong and important. We wanted to be strong and important.

"A drowning person will panic," he said. "They will do anything to stay above the water. That includes drowning the person who has come to save them. Do you understand?"

We nodded.

"Stay calm, protect yourself. That's lesson number one."

Our father, the maker of strange games, grabbed our little wrists and leapt into the pool. We still had our clothes on and sank quickly. Bubbles clouded the water, and I felt the weight of my tennis shoes. This was shocking, but I wasn't worried at first. Father had taught us to meditate and call him Sir. He had us stand on one foot for twenty minutes, and then switch. He had instructed us to hold, throw, twist, punch, and roll. We had recited passages from *The Art of War* and kicked his padded hands over and over and over. And we had also learned that a student trusted his master, that a son obeyed his father, but as the bubbles dissipated I saw Brandon fighting Father's grip.

That scared me. Was this a test? What if Father had gone insane? And as oxygen diminished I realized that punishment by Father was better than death. I decided to fight, too.

I hit Father with the empty hand, a *junzuki*, and a *hiki-te*. I *mae geri*-ed, gave him the *nidan geri* double kick and a *sando zuki* punch with my free arm. I gave a number three, three, three, with a *wado* to the neck. I gave him the *tate ken* vertical fist, an *uchi-uchi-utsu* combo to the gut, and then completed the sequence with a knee-scissor-cat-scratch—a move of my own invention. Nothing worked. Being underwater I couldn't gain enough force, and I began to think that there must be a whole separate study for underwater combat techniques. I imagined schools of ocean ninjas in scuba gear with blades for fins. I imagined a dojo master, capable of holding his breath for days, meditating cross-legged on a rainbow reef. But I didn't know underwater combat so I panicked, my fighting posture broke down, and I grew weak.

During the melee Brandon somehow managed to escape, and upon reaching the surface, did something remarkable: he dove back down and sunk his teeth into the enemy's hand. The attack surprised him so much he loosened his grip on me. This momentary freedom allowed me to propel myself off the bottom of the pool and land a head-butt deep into his groin. Bubbles sputtered from his mouth, and he curled into a ball. Gasping and exhausted, our faces already alive with tears, Brandon and I dragged ourselves out of the pool and ran.

Inside, Mother wrapped us in towels and rubbed our backs. Mom was the pilot light of our family, her love the steady glow that heated our home. But heat in summer wasn't good for much: "It's all right, boys," she said. "You know your father would never hurt you."

As if he'd been summoned, Father appeared at the door, dripping onto the hot pavement, and although we wouldn't look at him we knew he was there. We never got to lesson two.

I chose "Lesson One" after reading the anonymized shortlist of stories for a variety of reasons, but the main reason was the refusal to try and compress the conventional MFA-realist short story into a supershort format. This is what almost all of the other stories did, except for the one or two that tried to write the flash fiction form as a lyric poem (that is, keeping to a minimum of characterization and incident). Instead, the author practiced the flash fiction form with a nod toward its true ancestry, writing a piece that comes close to the parable. I cannot know for sure whether the author intended us to interpret "Lesson One" in a metaphysical or Kafkaesque light, but the makings of a dark parable are all there: the slightly inscrutable capital-F "Father," the "meditation" the two sons are made to practice, the mortally dangerous teaching method, the fighting moves taught by the Father that are then used against the Father (at this point, the "enemy"), the body of water, the caregiving Mother-figure, and the final mysterious refusal to look but knowing he (He) is there. . . . One could go on, but the author wisely didn't, creating a flash fiction that strikes like lightning, brief but illuminating. All this, and it was actually exciting to read."—Amit Majmudar, Final Judge, 2014 Able Muse Write Prize for Fiction on this winning story, "Lesson One," by J. Preston Witt.

Roy Bentley

"Squirrels on Skis" Star Performer Dies

Death can make an ocean look like it's a lot of endings,
but most of the time oceans are gorgeous with beginning.
Consider a tree squirrel who water skied in South Florida.
The treble trill of a radio-controlled boat's tinny engine
was its signal to let the shenanigans begin in earnest.

Though the performance wasn't like fine wine or food
you'd stand and applaud for, we stood. And applauded.
Fast forward a dozen or so years. I was still in Florida.
I'd dressed for the beach. Wore a Florida shirt, trunks.
Had my iPhone. Was scrolling the BBC news app.

There it was: *"Squirrels on Skis" Star Performer Dies.*
Turns out, the rodent-acrobat was a glutton for attention
and performed for snowbirds and busloads of tourists.
Figure eights to the driving beat of Lynyrd Skynyrd.
In the end, shaved areas of the scimitar-tail offered

access for a Tampa vet to administer chemotherapies.
Death came when it came to those huge brown eyes.
The next day, newsrooms all over the US and Canada
hummed with the footage of animal rights activists
tsk-tsking grandstands of approving hoots. Waves—

this fur-bearer flouted the waves, lived to be made
light of. Confounded armies of the overly logical.
How long a life? Long enough for thousands of
serial leaps toward the miraculous. Ah, the tug
of a tiny tow rope, face-fur luffing in the breeze!

Jeredith Merrin

The Burrowing Owl

    (Athene cunicularia)

In and out of

    fashion
    health
    favor.

        Or, in this case,
        burrows—

        these grassland and desert owls
        with legs like stilts:
        standing, surveying
        the flat land around them
        for beetles, scorpions, and other food.

In and out of

    shape
    humor
    tune.

        Busy squatters inhabiting
        abandoned holes of gopher,
        ground squirrel, tortoise,
        coyote, or fox;

    also, the tunnels of prairie dogs
    (more like prairie popcorn,
    that time I saw a colony,
    so quick and so many
    popping everywhere up & out).

In and out of

  order
  danger
  control.

    In breeding season the male
    sun-bleaches to buff
    from standing guard outside,
    while she stays cream and brown,
    keeping indoors with their young

    (clever owlets who scare intruders
    by hissing-rattling like snakes).

In and out of

  practice
  season
  focus.

    Yellow-eyed, white-eyebrowed.

In and out of

       trouble
       luck
       love.

              Endangered masters
              of exiting and entering—

like Marilyn in *The Misfits,*
up Clark Gable's makeshift
concrete-block steps and into
the half-built house in the desert,
then down again, and up, over
and over, exclaiming
(wholly given to the game):

"I can go in! And I can come out!"

How in their last movie
her ample body seems so fragile
as she goes break-your-heart
back and forth from happy to sad.

No one like her; but we do that, we all do.

Out of sorts. In heaven.
In a quandary. Out of time.

Jeredith Merrin

The Pharaoh Eagle Owl

(Bubo ascalaphus)

Look how it looks as it's looking
from an outcrop of rock:

buff, bleached rose, apricot,
blotched with dark and light—

sandstone rock, sandstone bird.

It could be carved *in situ*, like the sphinx.

What riddle is it posing,
large desert bird with deep orange eyes?

What secret are you keeping from yourself?

Fierce and monogamous, it has nested in the pyramids.

This is the owl of hidden-but-not-altogether;
this is the owl of figure-it-out.

By day, camouflaged in a crevice,
a hunter, tonight.

Hailey Leithauser

Rrribbit

So rarely does music
so clearly resemble
the creature who makes it.
Wrens and sparrows
sorrow larger,
the giant sloth,
goliath bird-
eating spider
cry out smaller
than they all are.
It's only the toad
consigned to her squat,
mud green, pot-shaped house,
fattening on flies,
who tries a nocturne
of such dense remorse
that it exhibits
commensurate size.

Hailey Leithauser

Sour Grapes

So you think you are sweet, full, nectarous?
You, who are acetous bladders, offal,
who on your high, risible trellis swell
bulbous as a toad, tumescing in must.

Someone told you that you were savory?
Lush, honey-ripe, scrumptious? You, stank globes,
you, who foul in the sun in gamy globs,
rank and wallow in a vinegar sea.

I would drink black lees, have a lawn grub squirm
across my tongue and nest my uvula,
would salt and swallow eel-and-kidney stew,

would favor wine—before I savored you—
of burr-thorn and a fine bacteria,
of bile, centipede, jimson weed and worm.

Hailey Leithauser

Triolet with Typewriter

> Kudos and glory to the quick brown fox,
> that mistress of Letters, famous forever,
> over dull Rover like a sly shuttlecock.
> Kudos! Glory to you, quickest of fox—
> Bring blight on the indolent canine, a pox
> on his house. Leap higher, live braver,
> for kudos, for glory! O quick brown fox,
> Mistress of Letters, famous forever.

Hailey Leithauser

The Hangman's Song

They say that heaven is sodden with light.
Heaven and Earth and six feet to go,
Earth and Heaven and ten little toes.

They say that Heaven is a doddering flight.
Earth and Heaven and in the space between
Heaven and Earth stays a creaking thing

made of air and wood and greasy string,
not owning sky, but getting close,
graupel and snow blown up his nose.

Pierre de Ronsard

Challenge for a Mounted Tournament in the Form of a Ballet

These entering knights send word that they are heir
to the River Meander, sons of the waters where
their fathers learned to guide and wheel their horses
just as Meander twists and turns in its courses.

Pyrrhus, in his armor, danced on Achilles'
grave in similar ways, and Aeneas, on Sicily's
shore, honored his father with tournaments
of war, directing a mounted dance of defense
where Trojan boys put stallions through their paces
in a hundred thousand martial interlaces.

Pallas trained these horses to the bit
and guides them currently with hand and wit;
she schooled them in her spirit with such skill
that by the bridle, they know the rider's will.

Observe them now as they curvet and dance,
retreat and step away; as they advance,
approach and come together. Like hails of darts,
first long, then short, playing their wartime parts
in a show of peace, they crisscross face to face,
obliquely or straight on, in the end to trace
a circle or a square, as if this were
a labyrinth where anyone might err
by straying onto paths that have no key—

as if they were dolphins dancing in the sea,
as if they were patterns formed by troops of cranes
against the blue and white of heaven's lanes.

*— Translated from the French[2] of Pierre de Ronsard [abridged]
by Terese Coe*

---

2   See "Translation Notes," *"Cartel pour le combat à cheval, en forme de balet"* on page 194 for the original French version.

Frank De Canio

Tough Customer

Compliance is a T-bone steak
dished up to whet the appetite
of someone it can barely slake
before he takes another bite.
Accommodation is the sauce
poured on the fear that seasons meat,
while pleas are lettuce that you toss
at him to make his meal complete.
And seeing you serve his behest
with such ingratiating mien,
he's quick to gobble up the rest
of it, until his plate is clean.
As tip, you'll find this patron's thrown
at you the masticated bone.

ABLE MUSE WRITE PRIZE FOR POETRY, 2014 ▪ WINNER

Scott M. Miller

Costanza e Preziosa

Portrait of Costanza Bonarelli, Gian Lorenzo Bernini, 1636 – 38.
"Model, Mistress, Muse. . . ." —*Sarah McPhee*

Dearest—	Beloved,
Though my body withers	from the bondage of this life,
my soul is unmoved;	I call out to you:
set me free and	see my faithless spirit run.
I will not fly. My	words alone are lighter than air;
purple wings are folded	like clay silted at river's edge,
tight below this	shirt clinging to sand and your
skirt. You caught my	breasts, your hands cupped, but no—
look—not my soul—	something even deeper—
the way my eyes turned to	something too close to the glare of the
open flame, how my hair,	untouchable, plummeting, jet-black,
leonine, became ambrosia	unfolding itself, newborn lizard brain,
rampart in the orchard	where no beast is named, nor tastes
of my neck. I am	the sun. I turn reptilian towards
she who now becomes	you, who now become
love and I come to hate	my only salvation:
my world, my life.	I swear I will leave her.
I swear I will never leave you.	On a cold afternoon you swam—recall?—
I carry a piece of the stone	I skipped across the waves that day, the place
in which you carved	a memory, fleet and unbearable:
me, lips parted, a slit	wide as the bounds of my desire,
leading into that perfect dark	where I know you always lie.

"The two-column poem, ideally made to be read straight across the columns as well as down one column and then the other, is notoriously difficult to compose. Almost always, its tour-de-force element overwhelms its subject and theme. Not so here. "Costanza e Preziosa" cries out to the reader. It sends us back to the famously scandalous sculpture by Bernini. Its passionate imagery—*that hair!*—reminds us of how each female lover can be, separately and together, "model, mistress, muse" and of how great passion sculpts the ages. Crafted with notable devotion, this is one of the finest ekphrastic poems I now know."—Dick Allen, Final Judge, 2014 Able Muse Write Prize (for Poetry) on this winning poem, "Costanza e Preziosa" by Scott M. Miller.

FICTION

Michael Lacare
Claire

I took the job because I was broke and because I was fortunate enough to be hired on the spot. An up and coming video chain, spreading across the country like a plague, with its vibrant blue and yellow logo, staking the hearts of the mom-and-pop shops, leaving the dead piled in great, heaping waves.

"Are you closing tonight?"

This was Claire Laskins. She was five feet six inches, slender with auburn hair that fell past her shoulders. She was nineteen, mild-mannered and had difficulty maintaining eye contact with me for more than a few seconds. She nervously played with her hands.

The store closed at midnight. Every night. Weekends too, including holidays. By the time we were done counting out our tills, vacuuming and shelving the returned video tapes, it was almost 1:15 a.m. before we walked out.

It was cold and Claire hadn't brought a coat. We stood outside the store, small white puffs of vapor leaving our mouths. She had her hands stuffed deep into the front pockets of her loose fitting khaki pants.

"Where'd you park?" I asked.

"My boyfriend is picking me up," she said.

I glanced at my watch.

"You can go ahead," she said. "You don't have to wait."

"I don't mind."

Claire shrugged. "Suit yourself."

"Do you like it so far?"

"This job?"

I nodded.

She thought about it for a second or two. "It's a job."

A police cruiser strolled past and the cop inside nodded in our direction.

"You want to hear something funny?" Claire said.

"Sure."

"When I first saw you, I thought you were one of the managers."

"Really?"

"I don't know why, but I did," she said.

"Do you go to school?" I asked.

Claire shook her head. "I want to, though. One day."

"What do you want to study?"

"Anything," she said.

Fifteen minutes later a green Chevy Nova pulled up to the curb. The windows were tinted making it difficult to see the driver.

"Gotta go." She pulled open the passenger door.

I caught a glimpse of the "boyfriend", the small patch of a tattoo on his forearm, his wrist resting limply on top of the steering wheel; his eyes focused on me, boring into me like lasers.

And then the door shut. I felt like he was still looking at me through the one-way glass.

The car screeched away.

So my parents sell the place we call home since I was four because the economy takes a shit and my father can't find work. This is 1989. Long Island. Somehow they believe Florida will be the answer to their prayers, and the next thing I know the moving truck is pulling up to the house and purging it of its contents.

Although my mother begs me to come with them, I politely decline, since I am in my freshman year as a film student at the School of Visual Arts in New York City, and there is nothing for me in Florida. It is a place of sunshine and beaches and palm trees, where postcards are plucked from convenience store racks depicting large women sitting in their ill-fitting bathing suits, sporting sunglasses, soaking up the sun, while above their heads, floats a dialogue bubble with the words, Having a whale of a time. Wish you were here.

On the day my parents get set to depart, my mother takes my face between her hands and says, "Are you sure you don't want to come with us?"

She gives me a peck on the cheek and presses me close to her, as though I am journeying off to war in a distant land.

It is my father's turn. He embraces me and the familiar scent of English Leather aftershave wafts into my nostrils. "We'll call when we get there," he says and pulls out a hundred dollar bill from his wallet. "Here. Just in case."

I watch the taillights of their Ford Taurus recede into traffic.

This is the first time I will be living on my own. I am officially an adult now.

Later that evening, as I am exiting the grocery store, I realize I've locked my keys in the car. I phone a locksmith. He charges me one hundred dollars.

My apartment is located precisely twelve minutes and thirty-seven seconds away from the video store, give or take, depending on traffic. I know this because I've timed it several times. It is a one-bedroom with hardwood floors and reeks of stale cigarette smoke. I do not smoke.

I have trouble sleeping and I write in my dairy until the red digits of the alarm clock flash 3:56 a.m., and as of today I dropped out of film school because I am convinced that it will not contribute in any way toward my career as a screenwriter.

The telephone rings.

"Hello?"

No answer.

"Hello."

Click.

It takes me another thirty-five minutes before I succumb to sleep.

Claire is checking in the returned tapes when I enter the store. She barely acknowledges me. The Store Manager, Sal, is working the register. The moment he lays eyes on me he says, "Michael, get over here and take over."

The trailer for the movie, *Ghost*, is playing on the monitors throughout the store. The part where Patrick Swayze is sitting behind Demi Moore as the pottery wheel comes on, Unchained Melody spills through the speakers, and I feel like puking because it runs on in an endless loop and I'm sick of it.

Claire keeps to herself for most of the night.

At the end of our shifts, I find her in the tiny break room, punching out.

"Hey," I say.

"Hey."

"Glad it wasn't so crazy busy tonight."

She flashes a half-smile, and then just like that Claire buries her face in her hands and begins to sob. It is the longest two minutes of my life. Finally, she grows silent and lifts her head up. Her eyes are red and swollen.

"I'm sorry," she says.

I do not know what to say.

Claire rises out of her seat and makes for the door.

"Wait," I say.

She freezes, but does not turn around. She stares at her shoes.

"Are you all right?"

"Nothing you need to worry about," she says and walks out.

It is 2:37 a.m. and I can hear my neighbors arguing in the apartment next door. The words, "Liar" and "You make me sick" are being tossed about, and then the sound of doors being slammed.

The telephone rings.

"Hello?"

No answer again. Breathing. Someone is there.

"Who is this?"

Click.

I leave the receiver off the hook.

I wake up on the living room floor, the sun shimmering in through the window. The receiver is resting beside me on the floor. I replace it and the moment I do, it rings.

I hesitate to lift it.

"Hello."

"Michael, it's Sal."

"Hey."

"Can you come to work a little earlier?"

"I guess—"

"See you at two," he says, cutting me off.

When I punch in, Sal follows me into the break room and says, "That fucking Ethan is fired. Second time he's called in."

Ethan is thirty-five and going through a divorce. The first time he calls in he tells Sal his wife slashed all the tires on his car.

"The excuse this time is that his wife slipped him a sleeping pill in his orange juice this morning and there's no way he can drive. Do you believe that? He's so full of shit."

I peer at the schedule pinned to the wall

and notice that Claire is not on it. "Claire not working tonight?"

"What? No." Sal walks back out onto the floor.

At the end of my shift, as I am walking back to my car, I look up and notice a vehicle with its headlights on parked on the other side of the lot. It is sitting there with its engine running.

I climb inside my car.

The other vehicle pulls away and I could have sworn it is a green Chevy Nova.

3:18 a.m. My neighbors are arguing again. Something smashes against the wall. I wonder what it is they are always arguing about. Should I call the police?

I stare at my phone. It rests on a tiny end table I purchased at Consumer's, but it wobbles because it is missing a screw.

When I wake up someone is knocking on my door. Two women with dark hair are smiling at me and holding out a pamphlet. Jehovah Witnesses. I take it and glance down at the words.

Can the dead really live again? Would you say .... Yes? No? Maybe? There is an illustration depicting a man and a woman, their backs to me, her head leaning against the man's shoulder. They are looking at a framed picture of what appears to be the little girl they recently lost hanging on the wall.

Still smiling, one of the women says, "Do you have a moment to talk to us?"

At the end of the night, Claire says, "Why did you ask me if I was going to school?"

"I don't know."

"Are you?"

"Film school," I say, not bothering to tell that I stopped going.

She looks up at me and flashes another one of her trademark half-smiles. She plays with her hands. "That's cool."

I tell her that I'd heard that LL Cool J had been a member here, before he moved out to California and made it big as a rapper. She nods and says, "Cool," again, and that she'd heard from one of the other employees that some of the Baldwin brothers were too, but not Alec.

I make a mental note to look them up in the computer.

We are standing outside and Claire's boyfriend is late picking her up. "Must have fallen asleep," she says. "He's always doing things like that."

"You can catch a ride with me," I say.

"I better not," she says and plops down on the edge of the curb. She picks up a pebble and traces faint figure eights into the sidewalk. "I'm sure he's on his way."

Almost forty minutes later, headlights turn into the plaza and the green Nova halts in front of us. Claire stands up, dusts off the back of her khaki and opens the door. She leaves without saying goodbye.

Sal walks out and locks the door. "What are you still doing here?"

"I was waiting for Claire's ride to come get her."

"Oh. I'm going to meet Barbara at the diner," Sal says. "You can meet us there if you want." Barbara was his girlfriend of almost ten years.

"Sure," I say, even though I don't really feel like it.

Although it is past 1:00 a.m., the diner is busy. Sal and Barbara (she reminds me of the actress Elizabeth Montgomery), are already there. Barbara is picking at a plate littered with French fries and gravy.

"Hey you," Barbara says and watches me slide into the booth across from them. Sal is holding a cigarette in between two fingers and blowing the smoke away from me.

"Ethan called me today," he says, "practically begging for his job back."

"You didn't give it to him, did you?" Barbara says.

Sal shrugs. "I don't know. I might."

"Jesus, Sal," she says.

I glance out the window. I think about telling them about Claire and how she broke down and cried in the store, but somehow it doesn't seem right.

By the time I get back to my apartment, it is almost 3:30 a.m. and the neighbors are at it again. The woman is screaming at the top of her lungs. When I open the door to my apartment, I scribble a note and affix it to the neighbor's door. It reads: Other people live here, you know.

At 3:47 a.m. my telephone rings. I do not answer it and it rings eight times before it stops.

I peer between the slats of the blinds. My view is that of the parking lot. As far as I can tell, no strange cars are idling. For now.

My clothes smell of smoke. I shed them and climb into the shower. While I'm in there I think I hear something.

I wait.

Nothing.

Just for the hell of it I call out, "Hello?" Then, "Is someone there?"

Sometimes I hate living alone.

Claire calls in sick to work today. Sal is not a happy camper.

"She's never called in before," I say in defense of her.

"I don't care," he says. "It's Friday and we're going to be slammed tonight."

Fridays and Saturdays are our busiest nights. The store usually rings up ten thousand dollars or more.

"What did she say?" I ask.

"She said she was sick."

"Did you try calling Ethan?"

Sal shoots me a look.

After work, Sal and I head to the diner again. Barbara is there and she is smoking a cigarette. "Busy?" she says.

"That's an understatement," Sal says and orders a Coke.

Forty-five minutes later, Sal picks up the check and I tell him I'll see him tomorrow.

"No you won't," he says. "I'm off."

"Lucky you."

"When you grow up someday to be a Store Manager," he says, "you can get a Saturday off too."

The heater in my car stops working and I tremble all the way back to my apartment. I end up having to park beside the dumpster and the aroma burns my nose.

While I'm fumbling for my keys, the neighbor's door opens. A tall man wearing a robe that has partially come undone is standing in the doorway. He is wearing tighty-whities.

"Hey," he says. "Did you put this note on my door?" In his hand is the piece of paper I used to write the message. "I'm asking you a question."

I find my keys and insert it into the lock. "No," I say and rush inside. I lean with my back against the door, my heart hammering against my chest. I peer through the peephole. He is standing right outside my door.

"Maybe you should mind your own business," he says and punches the door.

My mind is racing. Maybe now would be a good time to call the police. And then I think to myself that that would only aggravate the situation, so I let it ride.

I look through the peep hole again. He must have returned to his apartment because no one is there and his door is closed.

The following evening Claire is back at work.

"Hey," I say.

She looks at me. "Hey."

"What happened yesterday?"

"I was sick." A customer asks her where he can find a copy of *Blue Velvet*. Claire takes him to the film.

"Are you feeling better?" I ask.

"Yes," she says and wanders off.

I catch up with her in the documentary section, where she begins to straighten out the videocassettes.

"Someone keeps calling me," I say to her. "In the middle of the night, but they don't say anything when I answer."

"So?"

"It's weird."

A couple seconds pass before Claire says, "Maybe you should change your number."

Claire steps out of Sal's office. "Have a good night," she says.

"Wait for me," I say. "I'll walk out with you."

She turns to look at me. "I better wait alone this time."

Ten minutes later I walk outside and find Claire sitting on the curb again. "He's late again, huh?"

She glances at me but does not say anything. Her arms are clasped around her knees.

"Maybe he should invest in a watch," I say.

She looks away.

"I'm sorry, I didn't mean for that to come out the way it did."

"I don't want him to see you standing with me," she says. "Please, just go."

I am tempted to stay, but I don't know what this guy is capable of and so I concede. "See you tomorrow."

2:52 a.m. I'm awake and my thoughts drift to Claire. Is she in an abusive relationship? I wonder what they're like at home, how they interact. Do they spend their time arguing like my neighbors? I picture Claire as a wallflower, absorbing all his faults.

I have trouble falling back asleep. I jot down my thoughts about Claire and her boyfriend in my journal. I turn on the TV. I watch thirty minutes of a documentary about Mike Tyson's sudden rise in the boxing world. I swallow a second sleeping pill.

I hear a noise in the bathroom. I mute the television. I wait. The second sleeping pill is beginning to take its effect and I am scared to get up and look. Sometimes they make me hallucinate.

My eyes are slits and I don't remember the remote control falling out of my hand.

Is someone there? I want to call out, but it's like the words are frozen in my throat.

And then just as sleep embraces me, the door to my bathroom slowly closes.

In Sal's office, there is a two-drawer metal filing cabinet where the employee files are kept. Through the one-way glass, I can see Sal in the front of the store, talking on the phone.

I pull open the top drawer and quickly search for Claire's file. It's filed alphabetically by last name and she is just after mine. I quickly jot down her phone number.

An hour before she is due into work, I call from the telephone at the front of the store, next to the registers. The number has been disconnected.

Claire is late for work and when she arrives, Sal chastises her.

"I know," she says and, "I'm sorry."

"A call letting me know would have been nice," Sal says.

Claire does not tell him that her line has been disconnected. She spends the rest of the night shelving the returns. There are a lot of them.

Later I watch her go into the restroom. She does not come out for what seems like an eternity, and when she does her eyes are moist and red.

"Ever feel like the weight of the world is on your shoulders and you'd be better off dead?"

"Yes," I say.

She barely utters a word the remainder of the night.

The next day I notice that her hands are shaking as she punches in.

Sal is off today. We have a new assistant manager, who's been transferred from another store. His name is Wade and he spends the majority of his time in Sal's office, on the phone.

A uniformed police officer wanders into the store and begins to speak with Claire. They step outside. He is making notes on his pad.

When Claire walks back inside, she looks scared.

"Is everything okay?" I ask.

"They're fine," she says.

That's funny, I want to say. They don't look fine.

My neighbors have stopped arguing. At least, I have not heard them raising their voices in quite some time. When I return home one evening, there is a woman dressed in a black skirt and white blouse knocking on my door.

"Can I help you?"

She turns and looks at me. "I'm looking for Jodi."

"Jodi doesn't live there."

She seems confused. "Oh."

"I do," I say.

"That's funny. I was just here a couple of days ago."

"You must have the wrong place."

"Did you just move in?" she asks.

"No," I say. "I've been here for awhile."

Her brows furrow and she wrinkles her nose. "Are you sure?" Then she laughs and points at me. "Are you fucking with me?"

"No."

Her smile fades and I walk past her, shoving my key into the lock. "See?" I walk inside and close the door. I count to ten and peer through the peep hole. The woman is still there. She knocks on my door.

I answer it.

"Are you Bryan?" she asks.

Claire has called in again. Sal has the day off, so she lucked out because Wade could care less. He is in the back office, on the telephone.

The same police officer from the other day comes into the store and inquires about Claire. I tell him she called in. He then asks me if we have another way to get in touch with her.

"I'm sorry, we don't," I say.

"Let her know I stopped by," he says and walks out.

The next day when Claire returns to work I say, "That cop came by yesterday." She grabs a basket full of tapes. "Jesus," she says. "Really?"

I follow her to the Horror section. "Is everything cool?"

"The guy's a whack job."

"What do you mean?"

"Nothing," she says. "Forget it."

"The cop's a whack job?"

She rolls her eyes and sighs. We are now in the Drama section, which I find appropriate. "Big time."

"I don't get it," I say.

She sets the basket down. "The other day, I call the cops on my boyfriend and this whack-a-doodle comes out. He starts asking me all these questions and the next thing I know, he's as crazy as Billy."

"Billy?"

"My boyfriend."

"What happened?"

"I think the cop's stalking me," Claire says.

"No, what happened that you had to call the cops on your boyfriend?"

Claire hesitates and says nothing. Then she rolls up the sleeve on her left arm. There are several small, round singe marks on her skin.

"What are those?" I ask.

"Cigarette burns." She swallows hard, holding back tears. "It's something he does," she says, as if she is referring to a simple hobby, like stamp collecting or building model train sets.

"Jesus Christ." I am practically at a loss for words.

"It's not your problem," Claire says and heaves the basket toward New Releases. "Looks like I'm trading one psycho for another. Story of my life."

"What makes you say that?"

She turns to peer at me from over her shoulder. "Because he's relentless."

"What happened to your boyfriend?"

"He ran off," she says. "They're looking for him."

The cop is waiting for Claire when she gets off work. He is in his cruiser. She gets into the passenger seat and I watch them pull out of the parking lot.

Three days later, Claire informs me that her boyfriend has been arrested. He was caught hiding in a closet in his mother's house in Lindenhurst. She will have to testify against him in court.

I ask her how things are going with the officer.

She shrugs and says, "They're going."

Claire tells me that he finally left his wife, and that they have since moved in together into a tiny studio apartment across town, with tiled flooring and a view of the park.

"What's his name?" I ask.

"Ted," she says.

Ted has twin boys, age five.

A grin tips one corner of her mouth. "You want to hear something funny? He told me that he's in love."

I want to say things like, "This is sudden," or, "Sure feels like it's moving fast," or "Are you happy," but I don't.

"Crazy, right?" she says and shakes her head in disbelief.

Claire has not shown up for work in over a week. She has never updated her contact information, so there is no way to get in touch with her. Sal has written her off, especially since it is company policy to consider it job abandonment after three days.

Another week. Three weeks. Four.

No word from Claire. It is like she never existed. It's funny how you get to know certain people you work with, and then one day, they are gone and their faces begin to fade away.

Two months, three months, four.

Sal hires a new girl. Her name is Samantha. She is fifty-seven years old and originally from North Dakota. "The older ones are more responsible," Sal says.

Maybe, I think. Maybe not.

A friend of mine says I'll be able to rent a room at his house for half of what I am currently paying for my apartment. That's the good news. The bad news is that I have five months remaining on my existing lease. "Break it," he suggests. When I inquire about getting out of my lease early, the leasing agent tells me I'd still be responsible for all five months, plus I would lose my security deposit. They are so nice when you are contemplating renting, I think to myself, but so nasty on the way out.

I make plans to ditch the place in the middle of the night.

On the way home from work, a cop flips his lights on and pulls me over. I wait forever for the officer to get out of his vehicle, and when he does, I notice it is Ted.

"Hey," I say.

"License and registration, please," he says.

"Remember me? I used to work with Claire."

"License and registration," he says again.

I hand them to him. He uses a small flashlight to inspect the documents.

My stomach is in knots. "How's Claire?"

He glances at me, then at my paperwork and then back at me. "I wouldn't know," he says.

"What do you mean?"

"Claire left me."

"When?"

"Two and a half weeks after we moved in," Ted says. "I don't know where she went. Stay right here."

I watch him return to his vehicle. I wait as he checks my identification. I'm still not sure why he pulled me over.

When he finally makes his way back to me I say, "Did I do something wrong?"

He passes me my license and registration. "When you changed lanes back there, you failed to use your directional signal."

Really, because I think that I did. I always utilize my directional signal. Something tells me he is making this up. I am already having difficulty paying my auto insurance; a ticket would be the equivalent of a stake in my heart.

"By the way, those burn marks?" he says. "On her arm?"

Burn marks? Then I remember he is referring to Claire's scars, the ones made by Billy and his cigarettes.

"Yeah," I say.

"She did those to herself."

What is he talking about? How could she have possibly done that to herself? No one burns themselves with cigarettes.

"Are you sure?"

"She ain't all there," he says. "The girl's got issues." He tears the ticket from its pad. "You have thirty days to pay. The address is on the back where you can send in your payment, or you can go down directly to the clerk's office and pay it there."

Ted heads back to his cruiser. I toss the ticket onto the passenger seat. I wait for him to leave and then I pull back onto the street.

4:21 a.m. I have not been able to go back to sleep since the sound of the neighbors fighting again woke me. I eat a dish of ice cream and jot down a few lines in my journal. They are mostly about my earlier encounter with Ted. I could not, for the life of me, get out of my mind the things he said about Claire. Is it true? Had she burnt herself? Could she have been making those lies up about Billy? It's possible. What if Billy had been the victim all along? Wouldn't that be something?

And then it occurs to me that perhaps Ted's got it all wrong and he is bitter, and the only way he can feel better about the entire thing is if he spouts awful things about her. That's possible too.

The telephone rings.

Once, twice, three times.

"Hello?"

No answer.

"Claire?"

Dorie deWitt LaRue

To the Young Muslim Woman in Full Niqab on Motorcycle

The traffic's murderous instincts attest
to your skills of balance, poised as you are,
sidesaddle, not even holding on
to your husband, or brother, or father.
We lock eyes and for a few seconds
I could reach out of my taxi window
and touch the black blowing silk
and its tasteful bling.
Your azure painted nails and toes
match, the sandals fashionable
as a *Cosmo* girl's.
Perhaps underneath
you are wearing designer jeans,
with poems stuffed
into your pockets.
Perhaps there is a forbidden
paperback within the folds,
maybe *Reading Lolita,*
Catcher in the Rye.
Do you know how it feels to run
barefoot over new grass,
how the wind can touch
your face like the kiss of a lover
you have no intention of marrying?

Or did you complete the couplet's
last line and get to marry a prince?
If your veil froze,
would it make a shield?
Or would it crack
into a thousand pieces?
Above your full niqab those eyes,
those eyes have light in them.

Kathryn Locey

New Wine

I sip morning coffee on the patio,
admiring the sweet shear of my bermuda,
its fresh-cut smell, its level slope toward the fence.
Then, *drat,* I spot a pair of yellow weed-blooms,
dandelions—sprung up from nowhere,
or more likely springing back from being bent
by the mower wheel, not lopped by the blade.
Those pesky blowballs, whose roots dig in deep—
ground's so dry, I know I'll never rip them up
unless I use a trowel. But that would mean
setting down my coffee, launching myself
from the lawn chair, a trip to the shed for tools.
Sighing, I consider softening my stance
on these invaders. After all, it's the *back* yard—
not like neighbors along the street, the Reeds,
for instance, with their choreographed
shrubs and razor-edged driveway, will see
and think less of me. Just the Santoros
next door, who've erected a chicken coop
among the pines edging their property.
A rooster crowing at dawn startled me
at first but now blends with dogs yipping,
cars revving, trains whistling in the distance.
Besides, what's so bad about dandelions?
When I was little, I saw some growing

in the vacant lot next to our house,
thought them pretty flowers, picked a bouquet
for my mother. She thanked me but explained
the difference: *Dandelions are weeds,*
sweetheart. They grow wild—no stopping them
once we let them take hold. Yes, dandelions
spread and their skinny stems straggle,
but isn't it also true—some cooks
brew the roots, steam the leaves as greens,
even press the humble yellow petals
into wine?

Katharine Coles

Either They Were Human

Or they were not. Like us,
They wanted shelter.
Like us, they painted their walls
Once they had time to think of ornament, once

They wanted shelter
To be more than what it was.
Once, we had time to think of ornament; once
We too painted a wall

To be more than what it was,
With human figures and figures of beasts.
We too painted a wall
As if it could come alive

With human figures. The figures of beasts—
Remember how they danced
As if they could come alive
There on the stone. There in the flickering light

Remember how they danced,
Deer so light on their feet
There on the stone, there in the flickering light,
And the big cats wearing spots, chasing

Deer so light on their feet, so vivid
In our dreams they kept trading places
With the big cats. Wearing spots, they chased
First one then another

Into our dreams. They kept trading places.
Like us, they painted their walls,
First one, then the other.
They were not like us.

Catharine Savage Brosman

Departure

Six ocean-going cruise ships crowd the piers,
all sailing late this afternoon. We're last,
and least, among the thousands in arrears
with pleasure. Skies at noon were overcast,

but, to salute us, changed to *bleu marine,*
before imploding in a cloud of ash,
transpierced by scarlet light and notes of green—
soupçons of melancholy, with panache.

The air is mild. The sea's got patchy froth,
however, and it's swelling, even rough,
with fractured planes—old, sacerdotal cloth.
Perhaps it's molting, having had enough

of ancient skin, and self. It writhes and roils,
but thereby draws me more into the waves—
seductive, mortal danger. We're its spoils,
they say, its progeny, the jewel of caves

where elemental matter moved and churned,
compounded, multiplied—its being caught,
amazingly, for future sense—then turned,
in time, toward shore, and rudiments of thought.

We're swaying, as we enter the Gulf Stream.
What then in the Antarctic latitudes?
I'll give them all my courage, my esteem,
in homage to the world's primordial moods.

Catharine Savage Brosman

Sunny

In fifty-one, she danced the Charleston, well,
attired in a twenties frock, with fringe,
belonging to her mother, I suppose—
they had no money for new dresses (*who*
had money then, along the Rio Grande?)
She danced that night with Buddy Macintosh,
unprepossessing, but with lively feet.
He wore a beanie and a raccoon coat,

a hand-me-down from some distinguished man
who'd gone to Princeton. With her fringe and lace,
bedecked with retro necklaces, she charmed
us all, her heels kicked up, her hair awhirl,
as Buddy turned her deftly to the beat.
She went to college in New Mexico,
taught school, and drove a Thunderbird, her prize—
with style, and yet decorum. Many men

in that male world discerned her quality.
She chose one for his goodness, not his wealth.
Two sons came next. She barely aged, though—danced,
wore open sandals to preserve her toes
from deformation, kept house cleverly,
and made sun tea in jars, her namesake drink.
She greatly favored green. Through twenty years
of boys and men, her ivy dishes, chipped,

were still in use. One day, not quite by chance
(her husband casually gesturing),
she looked on a high shelf and found new green—
a set of pottery, the thought of love.
How years evaporate!—like rivulets
that die in desert sands, like rain above
the Organ Mountains, vanishing in air.
In time, she was unwell; her eyes played tricks,

her head ached; long siestas did no good.
She'd watch the evening gold and salmon play
across the sky and wonder if next year
she'd see them still. The illness grew in her,
the poisoned progeny, unnatural,
of her unwilling being. Finally
her thoughts became delusions, flickering,
then darkening, until the sun went out.

ABLE MUSE WRITE PRIZE FOR POETRY, 2014 ▪ FINALIST

Eric Berlin

For Lack of What Is Found

I am not convinced by the cartoon tooth
that hangs above the dentist's office door—
those wide glassy eyes, the bowlegged roots,
that gloved hand brandishing the brush, with a small
forced smile of its own like each tooth has teeth,
and those teeth have teeth—all bared for the love
of the sharp-edged tools that scour them clean.
I fell for the warmth of that smile once.

I have no sign except this blinding bulb
above my mattress, pelted by these moths
whose minor deaths cast shadows on my walls.
They sputter as they burn to paper pulp.
They celebrate one filament of light
as if they'd stumbled on the sun at night.

ESSAY

N.S. Thompson
Reading Donald Justice's "Lorca in California"

Lorca in California

1   Song of the State Troopers

Blue are the cycles,
Dark blue the helmets.
The blue sleeves shine
With the rainbows of oil slicks,
And why they don't cry is
Their hearts are leather
Their skulls are hard plastic.

They come up the roads.
By night they come,
Hunched over headlamps,
Leaving behind them
A silence of rubber
And small fears like beach sand
Ground underheel.
Look, concealed by their helmets
The vague outlines
Of pistols are forming.
They go by—let them pass.

O town of the moonflower,
Preserve of the orange
And the burst guava,
Let them pass!

2   Song of the Hours

Three cyclists pass under
Christina's window.
How far out she leans!
But tonight she ignores
The flowering goggles.
Tonight she sees nothing
Of fumes, of bandanas.
And the breeze of eight-thirty
Comes fumbling the curtain,
Clumsy, uncertain.
            [Pause: *guitar chord*.]
O, the scent of the lemons!

Two hikers pass under
Christina's window.
How far out she leans!
But tonight she ignores
The bronze of their torsos.
Tonight she hears nothing
Of radios, of sirens.
And the breeze of nine-thirty
Encircles her waist.
How cool it is, how chaste!
            [Pause: *guitar chord*.]
O, the bitter groves!

A young man stands under
Christina's window.
How far out she leans!
But tonight she ignores
The shadow in the shadow.
She hears and sees nothing
But night, the dark night.
And the breeze of ten-thirty
Comes up from the south,
Hot breath on her mouth.
            [Pause: *guitar chord*.]
O, the teeth of their branches!

★ ★ ★

This two-part poem comes from the new poems included in Donald Justice's *New and Selected Poems* (Knopf, 1995) and is a relatively late poem as well as a rather curious example of the poet's use of a prior text on which to create his "Platonic shadow," as he called the poems he created out of—or based on—a prior text. This was a technique often employed by the poet, who was extremely wide ranging in the texts he used and adapted. These could be anything from ancient Chinese text to poems by Weldon Kees, although his usual preference was for twentieth-century Hispanic poets, particularly César Vallejo and Rafael Alberti, both of these poets known for their experimental techniques, tending to Surrealism. And if the same can be said for their Spanish contemporary Federico García Lorca, who met and encouraged Vallejo in Madrid in the early 1930s, shortly before his own death in 1936 (Vallejo died shortly after in 1938), his poetry had deeper sources.

Unlike many experimental poets of the interwar years, Lorca was profoundly influenced by popular folk culture (where other poets used jazz, say) in the sense of a commitment to folklore and folk song, including his famous use of the *cante jondo* ("deep song") in the flamenco vocal tradition (see his *Poema del Cante Jondo*, 1921). In "Lorca in California" we see Donald Justice picking up on two of Lorca's folkloristic tinged poems, the first containing surreal imagery, and both hiding deeper meanings under a simple guise.

The title itself is interesting in that it combines a familiar name and puts that person or object in an unfamiliar setting, a pattern familiar since X.J. Kennedy's *Emily Dickinson in Southern California* (1973) and now seen with variations, as in titles like Billy Collins's "Shoveling Snow with Buddha." Although Lorca lived briefly in New York in 1929–1930, he never visited the West Coast, so it is strange to see him placed there. Obviously what Justice means here is Lorca *the poet* transferred to the Bear State, or rather his poems transformed and transferred there. Again, this was a typical method with the poet, which we can see again and again in his work. Not only does he "translate" a poem, but he changes its circumstances to another time and place, as in "Last Evening: At the Piano" after Rilke's "Letzer Abend" where the move is from mid-nineteenth-century Germany to twentieth-century America.

Thus in "Lorca in California" Justice boldly juxtaposes two Lorca texts written several years apart, although with a rural setting. The first section—"Song of the State Troopers"—takes as its starting point the opening sixteen lines of Lorca's "Romance de la Guardia Civil Española" (from *Primer Romancero Gitano,* 1924–1927), a "Song of the Spanish Civil Guard" which tells of the massacre of a town of gypsies by the feared paramilitary force that had been used with brutality to quell provincial unrest since its foundation in the nineteenth century. It is a poem that could well have offered a meta-narrative for, say, the atrocities occurring in Vietnam (as the film *Soldier Blue* had done in 1970), but Justice has candidly admitted his inability for sustained narrative and—despite many attempts—dramatic verse as well. In Lorca, the Civil Guard is a sinister brigade arriving by night and inhuman in that their skulls are lead ("de plomo las calaveras"), their souls are patent leather ("el alma de chabrol") and they give rise to fear wherever they go, using a difficult image of the sensation of fear that Lorca himself explained as the tingling feeling of sand trickling between the shoulder blades. This opening strophe ends with the surreal image of these troops that "hide a vague astronomy of unearthly pistols" in their heads ("occultan una vaga astronomía/ de pistolas inconcretas"):

> Los caballos negros son.
> Las herraduras son negras.
> Sobre las capas relucen
> manchas de tinta y de cera.
> Tienen, por eso no lloran,
> de plomo las calaveras.
> Con el alma de charol
> vienen por la carretera.
> Jorobados y nocturnos,
> por donde animan ordenan
> silencios de goma oscura
> y miedos de fina arena.
> Pasan, si quieren pasar,
> y ocultan en la cabeza
> una vaga astronomia
> de pistolas inconretas.

[Black are the horses. The horseshoes are black. Stains of dye and wax shine on the capes. The skulls are cast in lead, which is why they do not cry. With souls of patent leather, they come down the highway. Hunchbacked and nocturnal, wherever they appear, they command silence of dark rubber and fears of fine sand. They go wherever they will and hide in their heads a faint astronomy of vague pistols.]

By contrast with the Civil Guard on their black horses at night, the California Highway Patrolmen ride by on motorcycles, but they too are dehumanized by association with the uniform and their machines:

> Their hearts are leather
> Their skulls are hard plastic

They too give rise to "small fears like beach sand/ Ground underheel," and while they have no internal astronomy of pistols, the reader is enjoined to see what is in their heads:

> Look, concealed by their helmets
> The vague outlines
> Of pistols are forming.

At first this may not seem an effective image, if the reader takes the preposition in a locative sense (as "beside"), and perhaps the image could have been better put by choosing "in" or "inside" instead. Justice then departs completely from the source and concludes:

> They go by—let them pass!
>
> O town of the moonflower,
> Preserve of the orange
> And the burst guava,
> Let them pass!

This burst of exotic fruit and color contrasts so strikingly with the metallic troopers and their "rainbows of oil slicks" we can only conclude that they are extraneous to that peaceful exotic landscape; so alien and, indeed, unwanted that the poet declares "Let them pass!" The suggestion of menace in "burst guava" is a wonderful touch. Indeed, the poem works as a study in menace; ironically so, in that—like the Guardia Civil—this paramilitary force is also supposed to be occupied with maintaining law and order. But, also like them, it is called out in times of civil unrest, famously so in the 1970s. This part of the poem seems to suggest the disquiet a young Bohemian (a "hippy" at that time) might feel on seeing this show of state force riding by as he carries his stash of marijuana in the pocket of his jeans.

Also of note is the archaic inversion of several lines, mirroring the same in Lorca: "Los calallos negros son" becomes "Blue are the cycles," followed by "By night they come." Again, by harking back to old narrative schemata, these inversions add to the suggestion of menace.

The second section is a reworking of Lorca's early lyric from *Canciones* (1927) entitled "Arbolé, Arbolé" ("Tree, Tree") where the tree is first addressed (in an archaic form of the word) and we learn it is paradoxically both dry and green. The "dry" and "green" can refer to the outside and inside of the tree, its bark and its pith, but also to the bark and the green fruit of olives. Although not in stanzaic form, the poem is again in octosyllabic lines, as in the above *Romance,* with a good deal of assonantal rhyming:

> Arbolé, arbolé,
> seco y verdé.
>
> La niña del bello rostro
> está cogiendo aceituna.
> El viento, galán de torres,
> la prende por la cintura.
> Pasaron cuatro jinetes
> sobre jacas andaluzas,
> con trajes de azul y verde,
> con largas capas oscuras.
> "Vente a Córdoba, muchacha."
> La niña no los escucha.
> Pasaron tres torerillos
> delgaditos de cintura,
> con trajes color naranja
> y espadas de plata antigua.
> "Vente a Sevilla, muchacha."
> La niña no los escucha.
> Cuando la tarde se puso
> morada, con lux difusa,
> pasó un joven que llevaba
> rosas y mirtos de luna.
> "Vente a Granada, muchacha."
> Y la niña no lo escucha.
> La niña del bello rostro
> sigue cogiendo aceituna,
> con el brazo gris del viento
> ceñido por la cintura.
> Arbolé, arbolé.
> Seco y verdé.

[Tree, tree, dry and green. The girl with the pretty face is picking olives. The wind, "gallant of the towers," takes her round the waist. Four riders passed by on Andalusian ponies in blue and emerald costumes and long dark capes. "Come to Cordoba, *muchacha!*" The girl pays them no attention. Three narrow-waisted young bullfighters passed by with costumes of orange and swords of antique silver. "Come to Seville, *muchacha!*" The girl pays them no attention. When evening turned purple with suffused light, a young man passed by carrying roses and moonlike myrtle. "Come to Granada, *muchacha!*" And the girl pays no attention. The girl with the pretty face carries on picking olives with the wind's gray arm around her waist. Tree, tree. Dry and green.]

This song relates three scenes where young men try to tempt a young girl out picking olives to come with them to a big city, but she remains next to the tree held by the gray arm of the wind around her waist. This wind, the "galán de torres" (a gallant or suitor of towers), is traditionally personified in the *cante jondo* as a faithless lover, lifter of skirts and seducer, and the girl obviously prefers this "gallant of the towers" to the various young men, hence she is both "green" (ripe, available) and "dry" (barren, unavailable). It also juxtaposes the present tense of the girl's actions and responses with the past tense of the young men.

In "Song of the Hours" Justice makes use of three stanzas to individuate three separate times during the evening (eight-thirty, nine-thirty, ten-thirty) and cleverly uses word repetition ("under," "window," "leans!," "ignores," "nothing," then the hour) to bind the stanzas together formally, as in a sestina, followed by a rhyming couplet (curtain/certain, waist/chaste, south/mouth), ending with the pause for a guitar chord and the description of the lemon groves. In contrast to Lorca's *niña*, Christina appears to be trying to attract attention at the open window ("How far out she leans!") although she also ignores the young men. But Justice follows Lorca's poem in exploiting the opposition between the young men's gaudy attire and movement and the simple standing girl whose attraction is the natural beauty of her face, their colorful clothes and flowers juxtaposed with her everyday work. As in "Arbolé, arbolé," the young men are theatrically posed and dressed; the bikers in goggles and bandanas, the hikers showing off their torsos, while the third youth appears so shy and tongue-tied and love-struck he can only look at her from the shadows, unlike the more brazen guys. As the title suggests, Justice has given a tight temporal structure to the meetings, which take place at hourly intervals, but has added a progression after each encounter with the men: the breeze is first personified as a lover who is fumbling and uncertain, then one that manages to get an arm coolly around her waist, and finally one that is able to kiss her as it:

> Comes up from the south
> Hot breath on her mouth.

But there is a double irony here. It may be the sneaky breeze that is able to seduce Christina, but a further progression undercuts the first in the seductive scent of the lemons, then the bitterness of the groves and finally the "teeth of their branches," suggesting the potential danger of acrimony and physical aggression linked to the passions. Is there a subtle warning (as in countless folk songs) to Christina to beware of young men, both the show-offs and the shy? As it is, she appears dreamily associated with the breeze, unconscious of reality, happily ignoring the young men, but what will happen when she wants to taste the fruit?

In "Arbolé, arbolé" the busy young country girl with the beautiful face appears to be protected by the seductive wind as a rival suitor that actually holds on to her and prevents her from going off. In "Song of the Hours," the breeze is more dynamic, changing tactics until it gets what it wants.

Perhaps a final word should be said about the urban scene that Justice creates. One might expect the cliché of a quiet nocturnal scene, but the "fumes" and "the radios, sirens" are a brilliant reminder that this is not rural Spain, but a busy downtown area, albeit in a rural California with its lemon groves. Nevertheless, Christina "sees and hears nothing/But night, the dark night." Perhaps she does need the implied warning about the seductive breeze and the menacing lemon trees, introduced by that dramatic *rasgueado* guitar chord. A traditional theme in a very untraditional guise*: Come all ye fair and tender maidens, take warning how you court young men!*

★ ★ ★

The writer would like to thank Mrs. Jean Justice and Professor William Logan, executors of the Donald Justice estate, for permission to use this poem for critical purposes. "Lorca in California" is included in the poet's *Collected Poems,* Alfred A. Knopf, 2006.

INTERVIEW

R.S. Gwynn
Interviewed by Jason Phillip Reeser

Dogwatch

The North Atlantic, March 1944

The "happy time" is long past, and the great
Convoy steams eastward at nine knots to fill
Bellies of bombers and of boys whose fate
Will be to seek out other boys to kill.
Or be killed. Twenty-six, my father stands
The dogwatch, and he smokes and looks to sea,
Having this evening folded many hands
And held out for the right card patiently,
Raking a future in with bills and chips.
A flash, a muffled crack, and not much more,
And where, a moment since, one of our ships
Has been, more depths of darkness than before,
And, far behind, a home, a son, a wife,
And, waiting with them to be lived, a life.

Measure Press recently published R.S. Gwynn's latest collection of poetry, *Dogwatch*. I was fortunate enough to talk with him about the book. The author of *No Word of Farewell: Selected Poems 1970–2000,* and four previous collections, Gwynn is the editor of the *Pocket Anthology* series from Penguin Academics/Longman and *New Expansive Poetry*. He has taught at Lamar University since 1976, and lives in Beaumont, Texas.

◊ ◊ ◊ ◊

JPR: Let's get right to it. *Dogwatch*. The name, as a title, is a bit vague. I imagined it was some sort of modern, introspective terminology that only poets really understand. But the poem which bears the book's title, the fourth poem in the collection, is nothing of the kind. It is a wonderful view of a man at sea and at war. In the solitude of this "dogwatch," surrounded by death and the promise of more death to come, we get a glimpse of the promise of a man's life that is yet to be. There has to be a story behind this wonderful vignette. Can you share it with us?

RSG: I will, though I apologize for the long "back story." My father, after graduating from the University of North Carolina (where he had basically worked his way through, c. 1934–1938) was dismayed by a lot of the radical, pro-Soviet bombast there and obviously felt some kind of patriotic imperative. At the time UNC was more radical than Berkeley in the 1960s. I don't know all of his motives, but he signed up for pilot training in the Army Air Corps (as it was then known), was accepted, and went out to Randolph Field in San Antonio to train. For a kid from Leaksville, NC, San Antonio, as he often said, was an entirely different world. During his training, while walking punishment tours on the main pavilion, he had a heat stroke that put him in the infirmary for several days. This was, after all, rigorous training, with hazing, punishment tours, and other things that led to harsh reactions. I can imagine that he'd never experienced such heat as he met in San Antonio! I have written about this in a poem titled "Randolph Field, 1938," where I tried to imagine him stuck in the infirmary while his classmates advanced. Anyway, he wasn't able to graduate with his class and was offered a choice: start over with the next class or get an honorable discharge. He was terribly homesick and wanted to marry my mother, so he took the latter. Some years later he got his pilot's license and flew for several years until a bad experience in a storm front convinced him that he should give it up. I never flew with him, being very young at the time, but we did visit the local airstrip and looked at the planes. They were very romantic to me at a young age.

Anyway, he came back to NC, married my mom, Thelma Howe, and dabbled in several businesses, not very successfully. When WWII came along, he was not affected by the draft, having been already honorably discharged, and went down to Wilmington, NC, to work in the shipyards, which were involved in turning out Liberty Ships, and later Victory Ships, on a daily basis. He first worked as some kind of Safety Officer (probably because of his degree) but later decided to become a welder because of higher pay and overtime. The workers were housed in government-built duplexes (some of which may be standing today) and enjoyed a pretty good standard of living, what with rationing and all that entailed. My brother, Dallas, was born down there in 1943. There were several family members nearby, and they seemed to have a good life.

Nevertheless, late in 1943 he decided to apply for the Merchant Marine. Maybe this was wanderlust or some need to contribute to the war effort, I never knew. My mom and elder brother moved back to Leaksville, NC, and he went to train at Sheepshead Bay, NY. He emerged with a CPO ranking and served throughout the war on various ships, mostly going to Mediterranean ports like Oran and, later, Naples. They'd deliver war materials and ship back POWs. Daddy didn't care much for the Italian prisoners, whom he thought a bunch of slobs, but he always liked a ship full of German POWs, who kept discipline among themselves pretty well.

The incident in "Dogwatch" is basically fiction. He did go the North Atlantic route a couple of times, but his ships usually took the southern route. When he signed up, for whatever reason, the Battle of the Atlantic was pretty much won, so my depiction of his witnessing the sinking of a convoy ship is pretty much conjectural. Truthfully, he made a lot of money in poker games during this period, and he always told me that it was this money that allowed him to go into business after V-J Day. I don't mean in any way to downplay his service. He served, and he served honorably, even though he didn't have to. Some have mistakenly read "Dogwatch" as meaning that it was his ship that was hit. I hope that a careful reading will show that it was another ship and that he was luckily able to return home and start his "real" life.

JPR: No, I knew right away what you meant. At least for me, that was very clear.

RSG: If he'd gone down with a ship in 1944, it's obvious that I (b. 1948) wouldn't be here to answer your questions!

JPR: The very next poem, "348 S. Hamilton, 27288", is a perfect companion to "Dogwatch." Only this time, you are telling us about a life that has already been lived. We've just been through a death in our own family, and I had the feeling that you were with us as we went through the flotsam and jetsam of a loved one's life. It ends with these line: "Here are lists of bills to pay./ Here are footprints pressed in clay./ Here are the porcelain hands that pray./ Here are snapshots of the grave./ Here is one more thing to save./ Here is a life to clear away." Is this a catalog of an imagined life or is there a specific someone whose life you were describing?

RSG: No, not imagined. It's a poem about cleaning out my mother's house when she went into assisted living. Wisely, the house had been deeded years before to me and my two brothers, and we finally reached a decision that she couldn't live there in our childhood home any longer. My late elder brother had been mainly responsible for checking on her in her latter years, but he would occasionally show up to find food burning on the stove and Mom asleep during *Wheel of Fortune*. It was a matter of moving her, against her will, to assisted living or allowing her to remain in a dangerous situation. My wife and I got her dressed up in her Christmas outfit and took her to a good assisted facility over the holidays. Once she decided that she looked a lot better than any of the other women there, it was pretty much a done deal. She wasn't an especially vain person but liked to "look her best."

Once she was moved, the house had to be sold to support her. We chose an agent who would take the house and its possessions and sell them at auction. Over spring break, my wife Donna, my brother Andy, and I went through everything. We rented a 12x12 dumpster from the city to put everything in. She wasn't one of those obsessive pack rats you read about in the tabloids, but she had kept a lot of stuff over the years. We just about filled up the dumpster with things that had no use, keeping scrapbooks and other memorabilia. It was hard to decide what could be saved and what could be kept. But, yes, the poem is pretty accurate about what we found, most of it in her cedar chest.

JPR: In "Fancies and Contraries" you speak of the desire to be someone else. Not a specific person. Just someone other than who you are. If you weren't a poet, but say, a painter, or sculptor, or a novelist, who would you like to be?

RSG: Well, everyone has some kind of ideal alter ego. Sean Connery would be OK, but I guess, if you ask the question: painter: Magritte; sculptor: Brancusi; novelist: Hardy or Richard Yates. I knew Dick Yates a little, but wouldn't want to have had the pain of his life. Hardy and Larkin are my great masters, and I am so minor when compared to the great ones that I must fully apologize for my meager output over the years. I greatly admire Richard Wilbur, my first master, and the late Anthony Hecht, my second. And there are always those around who have had great, enduring careers like Joe Kennedy and Lew Turco. They have always been a guide and inspiration.

JPR: You may not be as minor as you think. Time will tell. And no matter that you feel compelled to apologize for your "meager output," the quality of the poetry in *Dogwatch* is such that you obviously keep your poetic skills honed.

RSG: Like a lot of contemporary poets, I teach for a living, in my case at Lamar University, where I've been since 1976. It's been a good place to teach, especially since we missed most of the "culture and theory" wars of the 1980s and 1990s that divided so many English departments, sometimes fatally. In one case I know of, a department split in two and ended up having a chair from the history department! For the last twenty years I've also been editor of the *Penguin Pocket Anthology* series from Pearson/Longman, and I've written at least one long piece of criticism for journals per year, most recently a piece for the *Hudson Review*. As for poetry, I write it when I feel moved to write it; sometimes these bursts of creativity go on for months at a time. I have been, however, somewhat lazy about sending out poems to journals; quite a few of the poems in *Dogwatch* have not been previously published, and it's been a dozen years since *No Word of Farewell,* my new and selected volume, came out. There are a lot of poets who seem to put out a new collection every year or so. More power to them. But I do think there's a lot of bad money that drives out good. I recently read a first book by George Green, who is the winner of this year's Poets' Prize. George is roughly my age, and this is his first collection.

JPR: Will *Dogwatch* be required reading in Mr. Gwynn's class next year?

RSG: No, I don't teach my own poems. Occasionally, I will show my students one of my poems as an example for an assignment.

JPR: So if you don't believe *Dogwatch* should be the topic of discussion in class, what should be?

RSG: I do believe that introduction to poetry writing courses should contain assignments that blend generic matters with appropriate formal choices; this week, for example, we are doing blank-verse dramatic monologues. We will "peer review" drafts tomorrow and present final versions on Thursday. I do believe in the collaborative process in making poems, which has stuck with me since my own graduate days. I want my entry-level students to learn both generic and formal choices. As I tell them, "We'll mainly be doing exercises in this course. If you want to proceed into the advanced workshop, maybe you'll have learned some directions to keep you from the direct expressions of personal complaints." I do think that kids (and these *are* basically kids from 18–20) need to learn this. I frankly wish that someone had told me this when I was at that age! I had to teach myself to write pentameter and sonnets.

JPR: You're known for your caustic wit and satire. Does that ever get you in trouble?

RSG: Years ago I wrote a mock-epic poem, *The Narcissiad,* which made fun of a lot of contemporary poets. Richard Wilbur gave a copy to his friend James Merrill, who was one of its main targets. I received a postcard from Merrill with a very funny quatrain meant to put me in my place. It did. But now I have a framed, fair copy of an unpublished poem by JM that may fetch a tidy sum some rainy day. I have had some trouble with negative reviews I've published. One resulted in a broken friendship, and another probably means that I'll never be reviewed by William Logan. I've been to AWP a total of three times, always afraid that I'd run into someone I gave a bad review. This did happen several years ago when I came face to face with a poet whom I'd known for a long time and her rather large husband. We were cordial, probably meaning she hadn't seen the review! Thank God for small favors. There are several folks out there whose paths I hope I'll never cross!

JPR: *Dogwatch* includes poems both sacred and secular. They work very well together.

RSG: The first poem in the book is titled "God's Secretary." It's about the woman who has to deal with all of the unanswered prayers that come in while working for a boss she's never even seen. The book contains poems on religious subjects, including a translation of Victor Hugo's *"Booz endormi,"* his retelling of the story of Ruth. It is a great poem, both sacred and secular, and I hope my version does it full honor. I do consider "Something of a Saint" to be a profoundly religious poem, contemplating how history's most famous but probably least-regarded stepfather, Joseph, dealt with the death of the man he claims as his own son, Jesus. For me, this is the most important poem about religious faith that I have ever written, but I also wrote it as a step-father who loves his boys. And I do retain some lapsed-Methodist faith, even though there's not a lot I find admirable these days about organized religion in the U.S. and elsewhere. However, my poems are mainly secular, even one titled "An Inaugural Prayer."

JPR: So many of the poems in this collection touch on aging and the mental and physical decline of the body: "Deposition in September," "Cruising to Byzantium," "Goldie Oldie," "Bloodwork," "Here the Sleepers," "Looney Tunes," and "Being & Nothingness" stand out on this subject. But I also love the image you leave us with at the end of your poem "Relict," of the older man who, in his mind, is stuck at 21. All these years you've been teaching, your students have remained a certain age. This age gap is always growing. How do you keep up with the younger generation, so that your approach to poetry can find common ground with theirs?

RSG: That's a tough question, personally and professionally, especially as one grows older. Facebook helps me to keep updated with certain aspects of pop culture, which are always helpful with younger students. With advanced and graduate students, it's not so much of a problem, for they expect to be evaluated at levels expected of English majors; with the "general requirements" sophomore lit classes, it requires a lot of work to keep abreast of where they are and what I can do to connect with them; even a reference to *NCIS,* for years the most popular series on TV, usually draws blank stares. I make my requirements in these courses very clear early on, so I don't expect much disagreement when they haven't come up to what I require, which really isn't much more than reading, taking some notes, and paying attention to the exam preps I give them. I have, perhaps, lowered my standards over these years a bit for these sophomore courses, and I've incorporated films, YouTube and other Internet bits as teaching aids. My main aim is not to be the gatekeeper but to help them proceed toward their degrees. I am not going to be the person who stops them because of a core curriculum course, unless they prove totally incompetent and do not do the work. They are not English majors, and I hope that they'll retain something, however small, from their last English course and will keep reading over the years.

JPR: Do you worry that without your flexibility they would simply blow off poetry and never look at it again?

RSG: I have no idea what my sophomore students will read in the future. So many college graduates never even read a novel again. But some of my sophomores do come to our poetry readings, are surprised by how much they've enjoyed the experience, and even buy the poets' books. My advanced poetry students, though, I hope will continue to read poems in their later lives. There's certainly not much of an audience for contemporary poetry, but if fairly well-educated adults happen to come across poems that they can understand, I'm happy. Anyway, those are the poems I try to write.

JPR: There is always discussion on how to keep (or create!) interest in poetry among younger people. Do you think this can only be done by connecting them to poets of their own generation? Or do you feel that if you present them with a solid foundation in the classics, it will lead them to find whichever poetry is right for them, whether it be classical or modern?

RSG: Both, I think. I have had advanced English students who have never read "Ode to a Nightingale," "Elegy Written in a Country Churchyard," or "A Valediction: Forbidding Mourning." So I teach these poems, especially to my writing students. But I teach my poetry students how to write rap and hip-hop, too. They always seem to get a kick out of hearing me rap to Langston Hughes's "Harlem Sweeties," and they get pretty animated performing their own lyrics.

JPR: Let's hope one of them gets your performance up on YouTube someday. Since we're both movie buffs, let me ask an odd question. If you could choose any actor from Hollywood, past or present, to record your poetry, who would it be? I'll help get you started by saying that I think William Holden would fit your poetry well. He has that same clever, charming yet biting wit for which you're known.

RSG: It's always Richard Burton, whose voice inspired me to be a poet. He was my hero early on, and he shall always be my hero. I first heard him at age fifteen, and I have never got over that voice.

JPR: Ah-ha! The Reverend T. Lawrence Shannon. A greatly troubled but brilliant performer. What was it you heard at fifteen? Don't tell me you saw him on stage. My envy would consume me.

RSG: My high school English class made a field trip to Greensboro to see his *Hamlet*, which was screened nationwide using a process called Electronovision. To use a cliché, I was blown away. That production is now available on DVD, and I highly recommend it. He was a great and foolish man, as are many, and a wonderful writer himself. One of the things in his memoirs is how, once he'd reached the age to play Lear, he was physically too weak to carry Cordelia's body. It's heartbreaking. What a Lear he could have given us! Instead we got *The Sandpiper*. There's an overlooked film he made for Fox early on called *Prince of Players*. He plays Edwin Booth. I must try to get a copy, now that I think of it.

JPR: What's next for you? Any projects on the horizon?

RSG: Now that I have mastered the use of our new Keurig, I can go on to finishing the 6th edition of *Literature: A Pocket Anthology*. Being the way I am, I'm generally looking forward to finishing a project, not beginning one! Besides, Donna and I have seven grandchildren to enjoy and some travel plans in the near future. Of course, there will always be the next poem, which will come from God knows where.

JPR: And just one last question. I know you are a dedicated Redskins fan. What do think their chances are of improving this season?

RSG: I remain eternally optimistic, as do most Cowboys fans.

ART & PHOTOGRAPHY

Adel Souto
Photography

Adel Souto is a Cuban-born artist, writer, and musician, currently living in Brooklyn, NY.

He has written for his own fanzines starting in the early 1990s, and has contributed pieces to numerous magazines, fanzines, and websites since. He has released several books, including a "best of" chapbook on the subject of a thirty-day vow of silence, and has also translated the works of Spanish poets.

Souto's work, both art pieces and photography, has been shown in galleries in NYC, Philadelphia, and Miami, as well as in Europe. His music videos have been screened at NYC's Anthology Film Archives, and he has lectured on the subject of occult influences in photography at the following NYU schools and departments: Steinhardt School of Culture, Education, and Human Development's Department of Art and Art Professions. Souto also produces the public access TV show, *Brooklyn's Alright If You Like Saxophones,* and is heavily involved with musical outfit 156, which has a handful of releases on several labels across the U.S.

CLEOPATRA'S NEEDLE

WALK ON BY

RIDE THE ISLAND

ESSAY

Michael Cohen
The Place Where It Happened

On a March morning recently I was following the S-turns of Golden Gate Road, ascending its ridges and sliding a little on its soft sand as it dipped into washes. I was just over the Tucson Mountains in Saguaro National Park. In my early college years at the University of Arizona, my friends and I would speed along these roads—all of them dirt then except the road to Ajo, joyriding in the middle of the night, hugging the inside of turns regardless of the possibility of oncoming traffic, sliding on sand and scree. We knew our young reflexes would save us from harm; in fact the practically deserted roads were the reason we survived.

This morning I was watching the roadside for flowers, but so far I'd been rewarded with only yellow brittlebush blossoms standing up from their low shrubs on taller stems and the pretty little stalks of orange flowers called globe mallow. Just as I was thinking that the paved roads would be better because of the runoff from the winter rains, a low hill opened on my left with patches of Mexican poppies, lupines, low pygmy daisies, white desert primrose, and many tiny wildflowers whose names I have never been able to remember, even though I've dutifully looked them up in a guide. Suddenly a small burst of bright color erupted on my right, just over the little dirt berm created by the road grader when it passed. Even at the creeping pace I was driving, the color went past before I could get a good look, so I stopped at a wider spot in the road, fifty yards on, put on my hazard blinkers, and walked back.

Plastic flowers surrounded a white cross upon whose horizontal piece, wider than its height, were the hand-printed letters of the name Dustin Jackson. The writer, who had printed the letters with a Magic Marker, had enclosed the name in quotation marks. A camo fatigue cap sat atop the cross, but most striking—and the note they struck for me was at first almost comic—were two

boots angled out from below the ends of the crosspiece. I wasn't sure whether they were Army-issue boots or biker's boots, but they were laced halfway up. A piece of what looked like a motorcycle's fender lay by itself on the dirt to the left.

After the first shock of those boots I could see well enough that this was a recent shrine or roadside memorial to a (probably) young man, perhaps in the military, who died recently as a result of a motorcycle accident on this spot. Growing up here in southern Arizona, visiting Mexico as I often did, I had seen many such memorials. This one was less elaborate than most, with no votive candles or mementoes left by friends or family. But a certain element of surprise always accompanies my coming upon these remembrances. I have been accustomed to ascribing it to culture shock: the shrines seem a part of grieving and remembering that is distinctively Latin and as common as Day of the Dead grave decoration. Thus another surprise awaited me when I got home that day and googled Dustin Jackson's name. He was thirty-six and a sergeant at Davis Monthan Air Force Base in Tucson, and he had recently returned from a tour of duty in Iraq—no surprises there. But Jackson was from Red Oak, Iowa, unmarried, and I looked in vain for a Hispanic name among his surviving family.

A little more googling brought me some general information about roadside shrines. Sylvia Grider, an anthropologist who has studied them, wrote in a *New York Times* article in 2009 that the custom of placing such memorials has spread from the American Southwest to the entire country. Apparently you don't have to be Hispanic to want to memorialize a dead family member or other loved one with this sort of shrine. But not everyone thinks it is a good idea to do so. In the blog that followed the *New York Times* article, one mother of a car accident victim wrote, "Grief is a private process. It needs to stay private." And another woman wrote, "I find them macabre."

One can't argue with an affective reaction like the second writer's. But the conviction of the first woman made me wonder. Does she mean that everyone's grief needs to stay private? Or is she simply asking, in another way, the question that used to occur to me: why do the shrine-makers feel a need to take their grief to the place where it happened?

★ ★ ★

A few miles outside of Tucson, on the road that leads to the town of Ajo and its huge but now inactive open-pit copper mine, is another memorial to a motorcycle rider. Much more elaborate than Dustin Jackson's, this one has an actual altar made of bricks, upon which are placed plastic flowers in vases, votive candles, a large bear fetish crudely carved from flagstone, two tiny orange traffic cones, various tokens of or models of motorcycles, and a three-foot high plaster angel festooned with flowers, rosary beads, crosses, and tiny motorcycle charms. A cross stands to the side of the altar with the name Donald spelled out in small letter tiles, the name of his motorcycle club, Southside M.C., and the years of his life, 1957–2004. A stanchion behind the altar holds up a small, solar powered garden light with a plastic blue jay wired to it, but what is most conspicuous is the motorcycle wheel supported two feet from the ground on a metal standard, with shining chrome spokes and a bright reflective hub. The rim of the wheel is bent out of round at the bottom, and black scuff marks mar the top of the whitewall trim. An aluminum strip around the standard identifies the motorcycle as a Harley-Davidson Heritage Softail.

Donald Borquez died here on D-Day in 2004, sixty years after the Normandy invasion but only forty-seven years after his birth. His memorial sits well back from the road, almost by an irrigation ditch that parallels Ajo Road, but that shining wheel in the air is readily visible as one approaches from either direction. The clearance from the road is an important issue in Tucson's regulation of roadside shrines. The state of Arizona has historically been permissive about the matter. Years ago when I was growing up here, the highway patrol itself set simple white wooden crosses at the sites of road fatalities. Sometime after I moved away to a teaching career in other states, the practice was discontinued, but families of accident victims then picked it up, placing either the crosses or more elaborate memorials at the sites. Tucson's regulation states simply that roadside memorials "may be left in place within the City of Tucson's rights-of-way as long as they are well maintained by others and do not pose a safety hazard or sight visibility issue."

★ ★ ★

From a distance you might mistake Kevin Robinson-Barajas's memorial for one of the "ghost bikes" that are sometimes seen in American cities and elsewhere in the world. According to the website ghostbikes.org, cyclists who die on city streets are sometimes commemorated by friends who paint a bike all white and lock it "to a street sign near the crash site, accompanied by a small plaque." There are now hundreds of these memorials throughout the world. But the ghost bikes have more than a personal remembrance for their purpose; they are reminders also of the danger cyclists always face in city streets. Though Kevin's memorial is at a busy Tucson intersection, it clearly is much more personal. And, as I stop at the Circle-K across the street and walk nearer, I can see that Kevin's bicycle is not white but blue, and festooned with plastic flowers and a tinsel wreath.

Kevin's bike remains upright because its back wheel is encased in Quikrete. On the leveled surface of the concrete is a stylized,

nearly life-sized Gila monster. The bike stands between standards that hold up a street light at one end and the traffic signals at the other. The intersection is that of Fort Lowell Road and Mountain Avenue, where a school bus struck and killed Kevin in September of 2008.

Near the back of Kevin's bicycle is a small group of rocks, some quite small and others as large as two feet on a side. A cross, vases of flowers, and votive candles are placed among the rocks. The blue and green hues of azurite and chrysocolla gleam from some of the rocks, obviously from a copper mine somewhere in the area. Others shine white in the sun, and when I look closer I see these are mostly quartz. Perhaps the rocks and the stylized lizard point to an interest in nature in the boy. One of the larger stones seems to be granite, not dressed or smoothed but engraved deeply on one irregular surface with these words:

Remember
Kevin Robinson-Barajas
age 15

★ ★ ★

This straightforward appeal to us may be the essence of this and other roadside shrines. They are conspicuous sites of the grief of families, certainly, but they also speak directly to the passersby and remind us to remember Kevin and remember, too, that we will also die. The reminder is seen by some as morbid; this word comes up often in the reactions of the shrines' critics.

"Why doesn't a memorial in a cemetery suffice?" is a question often asked by critics of the shrines. Those who make them have several responses to this question: a typical one is "this is where my loved one's spirit was last on earth." Another response is that the roadside site is in the land of the living, a place where the mourners can think of the dead loved one as actually having been, while the cemetery holds only remains, is a place of the dead, not a place in the world where he or she lived. These feelings are mixed, however, with the painful ones of remembering that the memorial marks where a death occurred.

Other critics of the memorials have trouble with such a public display of grief. "But, sure, the bravery of his grief did put me/ Into a towering passion," Hamlet says of Laertes's extravagant show of mourning at Ophelia's grave, and Hamlet is only one of many who are less than tolerant at such a show. Still other critics believe their objections are more logical. The 2009 *New York Times* article I mentioned also contains an attack on roadside shrines by a lawyer who some years ago successfully defended a client who had been sued for removing a roadside shrine. (Though many states tolerate the shrines, so far as I know only one, New Mexico, has a law protecting them.) The lawyer cited several reasons for not tolerating the shrines: in his view their presence amounts to a taking of public land for private purposes; he sees crosses, rosaries, and other religious tokens that are often part of the shrines as a violation of church-state separation; and he believes the shrines constitute a distraction and a hazard to drivers. Each of his points is contested many times by respondents to the *Times* blog.

★★★

On a July morning in 1998, my wife and I were driving along Interstate 40 toward Johnson City, Tennessee. Very early that morning we had been awakened by a telephone call from a hospital in Johnson City. During the night our younger son Dan had been involved in an accident on the stretch of I-40 we were now driving through. He had come upon an accident that had just happened. Pulling over to the side and turning on his hazard lights, he walked toward a car without lights, stopped on the roadway, partially blocking the passing lane. He moved around to the driver's side and was asking the man behind the wheel if he could help when a semi-trailer truck, moving away from the hazard lights on the right shoulder toward the inner lane, struck the stopped car on the passenger side, throwing Dan thirty feet into the highway median.

Miraculously, he was not killed. In fact no one died in either the first accident Dan had stopped for or in the truck's crashing into the already damaged car blocking the passing lane. Dan escaped without even a broken bone, though he was bruised all over and was unconscious for a brief time, waking up in the helicopter medevacing him to the Johnson City hospital. But he had no concussion, no fractures, and no internal injuries. He had called us from the emergency room after he had been thoroughly examined.

We were driving now to take him clothes—his had been cut off in the emergency room—and to take him to the auto yard where his car had been towed, now with a dead battery after its hazard lights blinked for many hours. As we drove we looked carefully along the road for any sign of the two accidents that had occurred somewhere there, in rapid succession, during the night. We could see no sign—no broken glass, no pieces of bumper, not even skid marks. We continued scanning the roadside until we were in the outskirts of Johnson City. And then, simultaneously, we both had the same thought. My wife gave voice to it: "If Dan had died there, we would know by now exactly where it happened. And we would never forget that spot of highway."

Gustavo Thomas

FEATURED ARTIST

Gustavo Thomas
A Photographic Exhibit

Travel has been my vice for almost twenty years. I came to photography through traveling the world. My first pictures began as simple visual documents of those trips. Eventually, I went beyond simple documents and began to travel with the purpose of creating photographs.

It has been an ongoing learning process—surely, nothing new—from planning where to visit, which subject to shoot, with which camera, what technique to use for processing these images, how to observe an event or space or person that crosses my path. I've learned to tune my sight and mind to the light, shapes, perspectives and to the attitudes of others. I've also learned that places and objects can—as people do—talk and have dialogues.

Nothing comes by itself. Everything I have collected along the way regularly comes together to show me an image that may not be the one I'm seeing at the moment, and right then, I know what it will become in the final stage.

Yes, I am a digital camera photographer. And I also work with image-editing programs, usually, digital art applications for tablets. I enjoy transforming all my photographs into what might be described as digital art.

I will keep on traveling, be it a walk through streets near home or through remote parts of the world. And in much the same way I've enjoyed traveling the world, now I also enjoy photographing it and transforming the images I shoot of it.

For me, photography will continue to be an exquisite journey.

★★★

Featured Art
F R O M **Gustavo Thomas**
★ ★ ★

A walker in Central Park

One one line, one one foot

Peggy's Cove BNW panorama

Figure near Sólfar

ON THE BRIDGE

National Monument of Scotland

Harmony

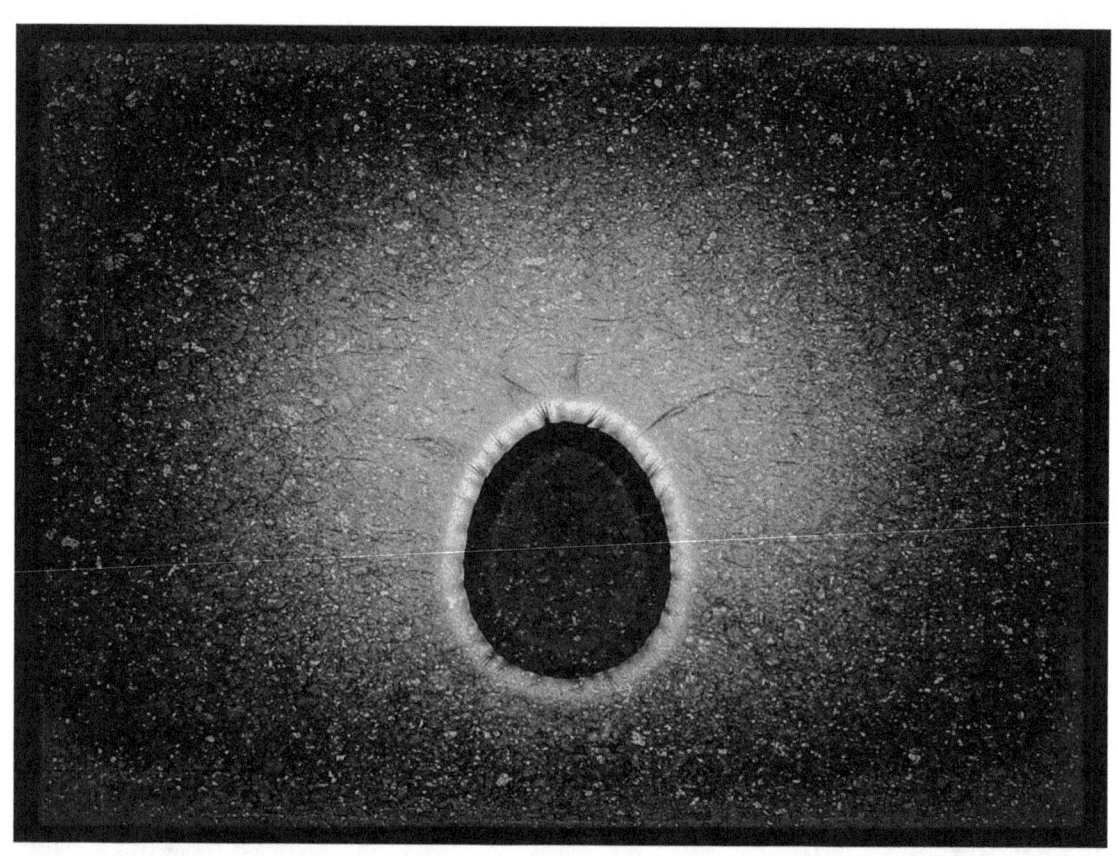

THE EGG

WATER STREET (OSAKA)

Sensō-ji During Sanja Matsuri

ESSAY

Barbara Haas
Crucible at Kronshtadt

The Gulf of Finland is one of those places on earth where the sky and sea coalesce so perfectly you disbelieve that you're still actually on earth and feel transported instead to an aqueous, cloud-draped, drizzly planet whose primary elements are those that create water in all its phases: frozen, liquid, vapor. The color palette in the Gulf partakes of the gray-to-silver spectrum. Veils of white often shroud the band where sea and sky meet. If it is a Tuesday morning and you are skiffing across the whitecaps in a Soviet-era aquabus, as I was last June, droplets stream in thin rivulets down the windows of the closed cabin, and everything beyond the glass washes together in a sea-splash miasma that has more to do with a submarine ride to Kronshtadt than a plodding but routine commuter transport out of Saint Petersburg.

The Gulf of Finland makes you doubt sunshine. The shore you've sailed from quickly evaporates behind you. Never mind that it is a celebrated shore in a storied city full of priceless Russian and European art, time-tested monuments, grand cathedrals, famous battle sites and the prison where Dostoevsky languished. The morning I made the trip, we chugged out of Neva Bay in full summer sun, but the Gulf of Finland, reliably swathed in mist, quickly swallowed us up. No matter what might be happening back in Saint Petersburg—revolution, bombardment, public executions, siege warfare, Shostakovich composing the Leningrad Symphony, Rasputin drowning in a canal—this was happening thirty nautical miles west of there: fog, rain, wind. Our creaky old aquabus had been making the passage to Kronshtadt long enough to practically groove a furrow through the moody Baltic chop. The horizon was not something I looked for.

I was the only person aboard with a video camera.

Everyone else seemed to have a targeted purpose for this trip: returning home after the night shift in Saint Petersburg, going to a day job on the island, couriers making a delivery, messengers riding over to pick something up.

Not that I lacked a targeted purpose myself . . . I was headed to the Saint Petersburg Dam, a state of the art specimen of contemporary technology built to hold back sea swells in the Gulf. Saint Petersburg had suffered 300 years of flooding, much of it the result of seiche waves, surface oscillations that swayed back and forth in long, standing rollers like water sloshed slowly to and fro in a bath tub. I wanted to see the cement and steel that had once and for all held back this environmental foe.

The Dam was a 25.4 kilometer structure that used Kotlin Island, where the fortress city of Kronshtadt stood, as an anchoring component in its flood barrier. It consisted of a 6.5-meter-high earthen embankment that bisected the Gulf, from north to south. Fifty-five million cubic yards of stone and soil had been hauled in to strengthen its foundation. This was buttressed with nearly three million cubic yards of reinforced cement. Running atop the Dam was a six-lane highway that linked up to the Saint Petersburg ring road. Two navigation channels on either side of Kronshtadt—one 300 meters wide, the other 100—made ship traffic possible between the Gulf and Neva Bay. These navigation channels were protected by huge steel gates kept in dry dock, and curved like gulls' wings. In the event of high water in the Baltic they could be floated into place and then sealed. With these gates shut, the dam made Neva Bay a closed reservoir.

This was both a blessing and a curse, like everything water related around Saint Petersburg. A bay is not a reservoir, for one thing—and a closed system was an environmental calamity in the making. The Neva River discharged the flow of a 300,000 kilometer watershed (about the size of the Chicago River). It was heavily tainted with agri-runoff and paper-mill chemicals from upstream sources, 28 percent of it left untreated. The hydrology in the area relied on currents in the Gulf of Finland to wash pollutants out to sea. With its gates closed, the Dam held back seiche waves that could deluge the city; true, but it also prevented any kind of natural mixing or exchange between the fresh waters of Neva Bay and the brackish ones of the Gulf. Already Bay-side biomes had degraded. The nutrient load entering the Gulf via the Neva River had a tendency to stagnate. This caused toxic blue-green algae to proliferate. Populations of filtering bivalves were in decline. So the Saint Petersburg Dam, for all its grandeur, innovation and justifiable acclaim, came preloaded with ecological controversy.

The windows in this aquabus had steamed up, and I cleared a small patch to look out. I had hoped to catch a glimpse of the Dam's stark and sleek white modules as we neared Kronshtadt. I had imagined that even from miles away its span would gleam impressively in the morning sun.

The morning sun. Ha ha.

Drizzly fog enveloped our aquabus so completely it was easy to believe there was no sun, no shore, no land out there anywhere at all. Navigation today was strictly by instruments. If instruments were to fail, faith and improvisation might have to take hold. I leaned my head against the window and considered my boat mates: the babushka in a headscarf, the middle-aged man with his belongings tidily stacked in a damp shopping bag tucked between his feet, the 20-something woman consulting her smartphone, whose ponytail bobbed with the rocking of the boat. A ponytail was not something I expected on the way to Kronshtadt—but why not? I had traveled in Russia long enough to rid myself of the preconceptions westerners bring to this formerly secretive and closed society. If ponytails had yet to fall for me, well why not now, why not here, bouncing on the frothy Gulf?

She fiddled with a couple of apps on her phone. She was the only person aboard this aquabus likely to know a little English, should I have a sudden urgent need to converse. We were headed to the sticks, Russian-style—beyond the tourist zone, beyond the cosmopolitan mix, beyond a place where anyone cared to engage with an American. What Boone, Iowa, was to Disneyland back in the States, for instance, Kronshtadt was to the Hermitage back in Saint Petersburg. Boone, Iowa, had hog confinements; its emphasis was on pork. Kronshtadt had the Baltic Fleet; its ships were armored with naval steel. If Kronshtadt bore any resemblance to Boone, Iowa, at all it was in this one thing: neither place embraced tourists.

Kronshtadt took things a step further. It was not about embracing.

This was the Russia where people sized you up fast and then just as quickly gave you their backs, a stiff social barrier every bit as foreboding as an embankment or a flood wall. Throughout history Kronshtadt had served as a stronghold and first line of defense against invaders from the west—the French, the Livonians, the British, the Nazis. After World War II it was designated a City of Military Glory for the "courage, endurance and heroism" exhibited there. That it could fulfill this role once more for the Motherland, not against a human invasion but a natural one, was significant. That an environmental enemy was the more pernicious was obvious: whenever water and people mixed it up in a battle for domain, people usually won out—but at considerable cost: financial, material and ecological. These victories were of the pyrrhic variety—from the Mississippi (rerouted at Atchafalaya) to Dauphin Island, Alabama (rebuilding of sand dunes after numerous hurricanes); from the Grand Coulee Dam on the Columbia River (decimation of salmon population, the "Ceremony of Tears") to the Dismal Swamp Canal at Chesapeake Bay.

In keeping with our notorious predilection for situating habitats in uninhabitable areas, Saint Petersburg was built on a shallow estuary. Of course it became the new capital of Russia under Peter the Great, who of course ordered sublime architectural wonders to be constructed in the floodplain and then of course filled those flood-prone wonders with rare art. Each time the Gulf of Finland came ashore and swamped the place, all this treasure had to be rescued. The Gulf had been coming ashore for millennia. It was an uncontainable wet beast, an unsustainably destructive neighbor for any city.

Serfs and slaves drove tree trunks down into the marshy fens and bogs. Massive granite blocks were then shipped from Finland. Prisoners of war from a victory over Sweden moved those blocks into place atop the tree trunks. Ten thousand laborers perished each month. Six rivers coursed through what would become the city proper at that time. In a move having as much to do with ecological sleight of hand as it did with mathematics, the six rivers were consolidated and reduced to three—the Neva, the Moika, the Fontanka. Saint Petersburg was inlaid with an elaborate network of canals. More granite, more deaths. The canals diverted river flow and controlled the rush of water to Neva Bay. Half of the bedrock of Finland served as causeways through which the rivers coursed. Palaces and cathedrals began to line these scenic waterways, and a jewel of a sparkling city took shape.

Saint Petersburg had been slowly sinking ever since, sinking beneath all that stone, the tree trunks and the granite sinking down into the natural morass below. No matter what a beloved tsar had once decreed, no matter how many slaves had toiled and died, or how much rock got brought in to shore up this mushy sponge of an estuary, the land (so-called) underneath Saint Petersburg knew that it was not land at all. It was a mire. Through regimes and revolutions and untold millions of rubles this never changed. Such was the formidable aspect of an environmental adversary that it could wait out the Russians. Even winter, a season that had always conferred such an advantage here against invasion, got nullified. No matter how biting the cold, no matter how much money was thrown at it, nature remained unmoved, unimpressed, unaltered.

The captain of the aquabus cut the engines for the No Wake Zone, and Ponytail pocketed her smartphone. We rocked toward port. The gauzy mist parted enough for me to see the rugged profile of a warship silhouetted against an ice-white sky, its gun barrels slanting upward. A few blocks beyond the docks the broad, high dome of the Naval Cathedral of St. Nicholas dominated the tree line. It was an imposing edifice of oxidized copper and braided gold leaf, a stronghold all its own. The cross atop the dome was gold encrusted and prominent, no doubt the first object visible to all incoming ships, perhaps even more noticeable than a guiding lighthouse. The Naval Cathedral accessorized well with the fortification theme of a place whose primary mission was to defend and repel. Kronshtadt's priorities had always been pretty simple. It had the isolation of a prison colony without ever having been one. Left to its own devices, alone in the mist, alone with the Gulf of Finland, it formed the nexus of three beguiling forces—God, war and water—almost too much for a small town like this to bear.

Just beyond the marina was a streetside depot where several city buses stood lined up. We filed off the boat, and I walked with the others through the drear. Most faces betrayed a certain hard set of the jaw, a nascent stoicism rigidified in the features, and I felt something ossifying into place like that for me. This harbor was frozen on average 160 days each year between December and April. Nobody worried about seiche waves then. The Gulf lay flat and tame beneath the weight of ice, as if hibernating. Until the six-lane highway atop the Dam got built, Kronshtadt was sometimes accessible in February only via ice-road trucking—or on cross-country skis. Winter kept the place pretty well cloistered.

The driver of the first bus I came to was leaning on the front bumper, taking a break. He cupped the coal of his cigarette against the drizzle and squinted through its smoke at me. I handed him the piece of paper on which I'd written "Saint Petersburg Dam" in Cyrillic. Traffic streamed steadily past the bus depot. The driver crushed his cigarette out on the wet pavement and walked to where he could see the cars splashing past. After a moment he stopped someone in a little green Mazda. He pointed at me, gestured somewhat in the direction of my video camera, and spoke familiarly to the driver, maybe a guy he knew.

This was often how it got done in Russia: someone knew someone, who showed up in a car. Other than at the airport, there were no taxi stands, not even around the hotels. When I needed to get to the Mariinsky Opera the other night, I told the bartender at the hotel. He escorted me out to the street, had me stand on the sidewalk while he stopped traffic, and eventually a pleasant fellow from Tajikistan agreed to drive me there. It was all very ad hoc.

I settled into the back of the little green Mazda, and we sped off.

We drove the northern arm of the Dam first, the longest span and the last portion completed. Although the project had begun in 1976 under Soviet leadership, it stalled during the collapse of the U.S.S.R. and didn't get restarted in earnest until Vladimir Putin came to power in 2000. He saw its completion in 2011, just in time for the gull-wing gates to swing into place and hold back a storm swell which, if it had happened the year before, might have ended up costing Saint Petersburg billions of rubles in damages. I settled back in the little green Mazda and considered this colossus.

The Dam resembled a heavily fortified bridge, and if you didn't know it was a flood barrier you might not guess. For 14 kilometers no one could exit this highway and no one could enter. The driver of the little green Mazda indulged himself a bit, changing lanes in graceful, luxurious arcs, occasionally darting between slower vehicles. The tires hissed against the smooth, wet pavement. A popular racing video game actually utilized this northern span for one of its competitive courses, and I had no problem at all imagining a dozen sports cars jockeying for position side by side in the lanes, swerving into each other, spinning out and flying off the roadway into the gray and obliterating Gulf waters below. My trip across it was Maserati-worthy. There was a seamless, high-velocity feel.

The Dam stood in stark defiance of everything we knew was impossible when it came to water. Guaranteed to protect against a hundred-year flood, it was the safest place on earth. I clutched the armrest and leaned forward. The safest place on earth didn't even look like earth, but a cloud-swept speedway melting into a soft mistiness at the edge of the world.

Four sluice gates were built into this northern span, each of them guarded here on top by a rampart-like barricade of cement. The driver pulled over in a service turnout near the first sluice gate so that I could shoot some video.

The sky was an ocean all its own, its vaguely delineated cloud shapes like wavelets skimming across the surface. These met an immense sea to the west that paradoxically resembled a sky with all the fog and low-hanging clouds. Dramatic veils draped down out of distant storm squalls like the trailing tendrils of sea creatures drifting through the murk. Every breath I drew came heavy with humidity and invited my lungs to remember a time when they weren't lungs at all but gills able to extract oxygen from water. Droplets clung to my hair, my hair clung to my face. Eventually my clothes felt pasted to my skin. Before long the sweater I had put on that morning was saturated and drooped from my shoulders. Water invaded everything. My Levi's hung heavily from my hips and refused to flex at the knees as I walked back to the little green Mazda. The wet denim worked against me. It pulled and dragged at my skin. An umbrella would have been irrelevant out here and ridiculous.

I weighed more in Kronshtadt at that moment than I had weighed when I boarded the aquabus in Saint Petersburg. Water was hitching a ride.

We drove the elegant roadway for an hour, charging back and forth, north to south. If I'd had anything to celebrate I might have felt like a conquering hero marking a major victory high atop the walls of a castle keep. This wasn't a victory, though, and there were no heroics. The wind and rain so limited my visibility I knew none of the video footage would come out. My heart sank when I previewed some of it, the frames watery and indistinct. Where the sky should be I saw a silvery panorama that appeared to be dissolving. Looking on, I almost wanted to shake like a dog does after a bath. Even when I thought I had set up a beautiful shot—and a clear one, to boot—a gust apparently blew through, and spattered the lens with rain. Water infused everything out there.

On the Dam's nether arm, the span south of Kronshtadt, the highway dropped twenty-eight meters beneath the level of the water into a tunnel twelve kilometers long and six-lanes wide that lay below the sediment bed of the Gulf. The tunnel ran under the broader of the two navigation channels. Up above, at the water's surface, ships could steam into Neva Bay at will without waiting for a drawbridge or a liftgate and then steam back out. Down below, beneath the seafloor, Omega chambers had been painstakingly locked into place one after the other to form the tunnel through which vehicular traffic coursed nonstop.

Naturally, the technology during the time of Peter the Great was different than now, not to mention the labor pool (no serfs or slaves), but when it came to dealing with water the thought process was the same: block, redirect, channel, impede. The Dam made sense. Everything about it was orderly, logical, well planned. A technological bulwark, it bore the stamp of human ingenuity.

Surrounded by a fog that appeared to be shielding the sluice gates on all sides, lest there be a breach, the Dam faced off against a brooding, restless, shape-shifting water empire out in the Gulf that was neither subject to reason nor governed by it. No matter the century or what the status of earthbound engineering, logic and planning could not touch it. Seeing the two of them together, the water empire and the Dam, drove this point home. One was constructed, fixed, sturdily entrenched, precise—at once aesthetically pleasing and invaluably useful. The other was inexact and raw, loose and free, not a thing at all but a force. It had always found a way to prevail. Even a City of Military Glory like Kronshtadt had no answer for it ultimately.

Of course, everything was holding steady today. Today the Gulf of Finland was on its best behavior, pretending that it was a housebroken kind of mind-your-manners body of water, docile like Lake Mead.

But something in its ability to turn the sea into sky and then the sky into a hovering opaque world above us made me wary about what might be incubating out there, biding its time, gathering strength, using the place as a crucible for tempering itself, and then waiting, holding back until something materialized, delaying, delaying, casually casting about for an opening. Then it would do what water always did when it found one. It would surge on through.

Rain washed down the sides of the Mazda, and we exited the Dam's million-ruble highway to wend our way along the more mundane, tree-lined streets of Kronshtadt back toward the military harbor and the waiting aquabus. My driver slowed before a broad plaza of neatly laid stone, then pulled over to the curb and put on the parking brake. I rubbed condensation from the window and peered out. Guarded on two sides by trim canals and presiding over the plaza was the Naval Cathedral, a thickset, meticulously-cut structure with the frightful density of solid block. Its well-measured corners—squared, true and perfectly aligned—exuded a type of calculus and confidence that told of something that expected to outlast the Gulf of Finland.

My driver pointed through the windshield at it and toward my video camera.

"I should shoot some footage?" I held my camera up.

"Da," he said, looking into the rain. The sky framed the Naval Cathedral on one side, gray and somber. His profile framed it on the other—firm, determined lines from brow to chin that allowed me to read an expression of satisfied pride on his face. He gazed upon Kronshtadt's crowning achievement, and he nodded. "Da."

It was touching.

He had taken me to the Dam and probably even raised an eyebrow once or twice as to why I, a tourist from the west, would wish to see it, knowing maybe there wouldn't be very much to see. *Would I come away disappointed? Would it be a waste of time? Besides which—who comes to Russia to look at a dam?* Now he wanted to make sure I spent some quality time with his town's truly glorious claim to fame, a monument every bit as worthy and eye-catching in its own right as anything in Saint Petersburg.

Your average seed-corn cap-wearing good ol' boy driving a pickup truck back in Boone, Iowa, might lift an eyebrow, too, if a middle-aged Russian woman who spoke little English wanted to visit the county grain elevator, for instance, and shoot an hour's worth of inconsequential video footage there. He would puzzle over her request but politely oblige. After the grain elevator, though, after the excursion with nothing much to see, he would drive her down Mamie Eisenhower Avenue, Boone's sole touristy strip, and he'd pull up beside Goldie's Diner, whose deep-fried tenderloins had been voted best in the state since 2009.

Kronshtadt had God.

Boone, Iowa, pork.

Not that the two were mutually exclusive. . . .

But pork never prompted exaltation, never inspired the building of a cathedral or stirred anyone to such heights, never narrated its splendor in stained-glass windows or demanded curlicue flourishes of gold leaf.

Kronshtadt had God *plus* war *plus* water. It had been saddled with sobering obligations and did not ultimately resemble Boone, Iowa, at all.

A city like Kronshtadt was always walling something in, walling something out, hoisting stone, hauling in cement, forging steel, installing ramparts, commanding natural resources to hold restless forces at bay and keeping watch, always vigilant.

I stood in the rain and zoomed my camera in for a tight shot. Gold anchors, gold oars, gold life preservers. This lacy design formed a necklace along the crest of the cathedral's broad dome, a filigree of color, light and nautical shapes that drew my lens upward to the heavens. My last shot ended there in a white ocean, a blur of fog and rain where the sky must surely be.

ABLE MUSE WRITE PRIZE FOR POETRY, 2014 ▪ FINALIST

Marilyn L. Taylor

River II: Accidental Reflection

> *On the lower sheet [of my painting], the left-most image was printed down. River II preserves this accidental reflection.*
> —Ellsworth Kelly

An accident, was it? Reflections often are
precisely that: little glints of clarity
in a wash of ruffled chaos—like a star
winking and sputtering unimpressively
behind the curtain of competing light
that we call *ambient*. And this is how
you realized a way to recreate
the chronicles of rivers: upside down,
purling backward, puckering a skein
of water with your brushes, showing where
a wrinkle on the surface might explain
the rocks below. But only here and there—
reflecting, in your enigmatic way,
what rivers might or might not have to say.

J.P. Grasser

Gyroscope

After Howard Nemerov

Pirouetting inside its iron globe
like the compass needle that can't find North,
the contraption whirs across linoleum
in memory. It's useless now, rendered
obsolete without the thread—frayed, cut short
by years of force. Have they balanced your
lithium levels? How long since you slept
on the kitchen floor? Since we spoke? Faster,
its insides become all light, negative
space, tricking the eye into clear belief
that solid might pass through solid, like spokes
on a wheel. I am sorry for this guile,
guideless wandering through days. The center
screeches across tile, winds down, falls finally
back into its cage.

Zara Raab

The Sere, the Yellow Leaf

Old friends I loved the best
are preparing for my death,
setting out the winding cloth.
It's in their eyes, and so I ready
myself, looking back, and tidy
a life and measure its worth.

A weasel child, I was drilled
in honesty and fortitude,
begot of Germans and Scots,
of Devon and County Cork.
Will they say his was bad stock,
or he knew not what he made?

Will they say he had no friend?
That a chill held him apart,
that his dreams came to end
in pain and ruin and divorce,
that he was foolish, or worse,
that ambition grilled his heart?

Don't let it be said I don't respect
a stranger's care, his kindness:
In thanks, I say, please inspect
me before burial, as we check
before sleep, the feet and neck
for the ache that may trouble us.

FICTION

Bridget Apfeld
Water Deep, Cold

The summer before last, the annual canoeing trip: eight of us jammed into someone's cousin's friend's van for ten hours, legs cramping and wrappers everywhere, faces pressed against the windows to sleep, and somebody had spilled soda on the back seat but if we cleaned it fast enough you'd never know it. Three of my girlfriends and two boyfriends and a boy we all claimed as a friend, plus an extra boy who was a second cousin, or a friend from over the state line—the details were unimportant—and anyway he chipped in gas money and brought his own gear. Near six hundred miles of black pine and sudden rain showers that raised mist and made the road slick and greasy, and we pulled into the outfitters' lot an hour before dusk. We slapped at mosquitos and joked about bears and argued over who got the only bed in the humid bunkhouse room where we would sleep before our river drop-off the next morning. The bathrooms were hot and spiders crawled in the sinks but we shrieked happily in the cold shower spray and reminded ourselves this was *our last real shower, guys,* before a week of dirt.

Should we split up? Sarah asked when we jostled over the few maps in the bunkroom, our damp heads dripping onto the mattress pads that reeked of mildew.

Stay together, Emily and Jess said.

Split up, their boyfriends said together, ulterior motives on their mind, and high-fived.

Gross, Steph said. Everyone rolled their eyes.

We can decide at the drop-off, I said, and it was then that we remembered the dawn send-off and the ten hours we'd spent in the van, so we unzipped our sleeping bags, and we hunched up close together, then spread out when we got too hot, then panicked a bit about the dark corners in the room and bunched up once more, and whispered about the prospect of bears again, and slept.

We separated after the outfitters hauled us out to a slow bend in the river chain, where we could either follow the water through the open rice marsh into the lakes, or keep on in the pine shadow where the rivers trailed into more rivers and the muskrats kept the banks shiny with mud. I went toward the lakes with three others, Emily and Jake, and the unknown boy, Sam. Four was a good number and we skimmed through the rice quietly. The itchy reeds dropped seed into the canoes and grabbed at our arms, and craning our heads out over the marsh we could see nothing but golden fields of grain, waving, hissing. Grasshoppers leapt from stalk to stalk and if one hit you mid-jump it clung fiercely until you plucked it off and flung it back into the mess of wisped and cracked stalks. It was hot and our arms burned in the sun and sweat dripped down our noses but we did not break stride until we shot from the rice marsh and watched the reeds close behind us, obscuring our trail, and the water grew dark around us and we faced the entry to the lakes: bluffs, gray, closed above us, and we skirted through the narrow mouth and passed into the deep water country.

Sam was behind me in the stern and rested his paddle on the gunwale.

Old here, he said.

Yes, I said, not knowing what else to say.

It's nice, he said.

We should keep going, I said, and dipped hard into the water even though it meant a faster pace, and we soon passed the second canoe with our speed, and laughed at Emily and Jake's frustration as they sweated to keep up, laughed so loud I thought the deer on the distant shore would prick up their ears and scatter, whitetails leaping into the gloom.

The first night we could catch no fish so Emily and I pumped water to boil and the boys ripped open bags of dehydrated corn, spilling most in the grass, and I frowned when I thought of the animal visitors we could expect from that.

Sam is nice, Emily said, like she wanted to convince me.

I know that, I said. We crouched on the rocks in silence for a bit, and I grabbed her hand and squeezed when a snapper raised its head.

Here for the fish bones, she said, and we watched it sink away.

Jake wants me to move in, Emily said, and I looked at her quick but she had turned her face and in the dusk I could not see it well.

Do you want to? I asked.

It would be nice to be married. It would mean security, she said.

He asked you to marry him? I asked. I splashed water from the bottle and shook out the filter tubing.

It's sort of a given, she said, and anyway, it's too late to start over.

You're twenty-one, I said.

I know, she said, sad, and stood up and stretched her arms behind her.

The gravel behind us skittered and we turned to see Sam picking his way down to the shore. He was tall and ducked out from the brush awkwardly, like he didn't want it to touch him at all.

Fire's on, he said.

Thank God, Emily said, and we stepped carefully up the rocks to the campsite.

Rain the next day, rain that met the lake like it was going up instead of down, that made the frogs jump in the shallows and the walleye rise to the surface so that you bumped them with your paddle and they just rolled there, lazy, bloated on shiners and perch. We stayed close to the lake edges and watched for lightning. I crouched in the bow and Emily had the stern today and we followed the boys' canoe slowly, some distance behind so that with their hoods pulled up you couldn't tell which was which.

Far off, thunder—maybe miles away. But we both heard it so we stopped our stroke and dug in hard starboard and let the canoe drift into the clotted roots on the shoreline. We balanced carefully now because flipping meant losing everything down the silty shelf and it was difficult to keep still with the canoe rocking against the branches and rocks that jumbled up together. The roots were slippery with algae and moss and Emily couldn't keep a grip when she tried to anchor the stern.

Don't bother, I said, and she sniffed, which I knew meant she was tired and too cold.

I wedged my paddle along the ribs and carefully turned so we were facing each other. Her hands were pruney and clutched her paddle tight.

We'll stop soon, I said.

Will they come back to find us? she asked.

Do they need to? I asked. She said nothing and I turned back to the bow.

When there was a break in the rain we hit a stride fast and breathed easier with the wake flowing strong behind us, and we crossed into the center of the lake to follow the patterns of the deeper water. We passed over black patches where the wind shadowed the waves and watched loons dive for perch.

Running up into the shallows of the island where we had planned to spend the night, the smell of rain and fog was thick in the air, but clean, like cut grass. The boys were there and had pitched the tent, and now struggled to anchor the bear bag.

Get lost? Sam asked.

Don't be stupid, Emily said. He looked at me and I shook my head.

Baby, Jake said, and she smiled that small smile of hers she only saved for when she wanted something.

She didn't want you to rescue us, Emily said. I stared. Jake laughed.

Tough one, Sam said, and I felt like I had to say something so I said, not really.

Emily moved up near Jake and asked him to show her how to tie a slip knot and I could tell I would not want to listen, so I moved off to the fire grate and checked how damp it was. Rain dripped off the trees and made the pine needles stick together in clumps and when I knelt and brushed them aside the dirt was moist and spotted with woodlice and daddy longlegs.

A shadow above me; Sam's shoes approached my right knee and stopped.

Rainy today, he said.

Sure, I said. He jostled a stand of maidenhair with his shoe and the fronds pulled at his laces. He kicked them loose and coughed.

Did you really not want us to come back for you? he asked.

I didn't really care, I said, and he walked away.

Late in the black night I woke and listened hard for whatever had startled me out of sleep. Emily curled next to me in the tiny two-man and breathed drily through her nose. I lay on my back with my eyes shut, picking apart the noises outside: rattle of mice under the dry leaves; scratching on the tent siding, an overhanging branch; the thick bump of giant moths feeling their way across rotting stumps. A fish jumped in the lake, heavy, and the night waves did not silence the slight rasp when the cormorant slipped into the water behind it. The boys wheezed in their tent a few yards downwind and I strained to hear the slow shamble in the brush that made my heart beat uncomfortably fast, the chuffing of hot breath over teeth, but there was nothing I could hear above the pines moaning as their roots inched down, into deep earth and deep rock, so I turned over and slept lightly until dawn.

It was long in the morning the next day when we hit the half-mile portage, and our arms were heavy and stiff, so when we saw the shallow stream that bypassed straight into the next lake there was quick argument about taking the shortcut.

We can walk it, Emily said, it's shallow, look.

You'll carry the canoes if they get grounded, then? I asked.

Ten minutes versus an hour, Sam said.

Then Emily crossed her arms and Jake saw it so the argument was over, and we splashed out of the canoes awkwardly and felt out our footing for the walk down the stream. We all winced with the first soaking of our shoes but soon the cold water felt good on our feet and we paid less attention to pebbles scraping the canoe bottoms, and even laughed at a tricky point where we could barely drag the canoes through, when we saw dry glacier rock rise up into beige banks and the river narrowed into a thread.

Then when the stream became wide and the sun glared off the higher water, Jake let go of the bow and walked to a jutted-out boulder, long and flat.

What are you doing? I called. Our canoe drifted randomly and I felt the current tug it from below.

Look what I found, he said, and held up a buck skull. He gripped the rack in both hands and raised it above his head, grinning.

Sweet, Sam said, and he and Emily pulled closer. Sam left their canoe and climbed up onto the boulder and the two boys turned the bone over and over between themselves, excited.

That's really gross, Emily said, and they laughed at her.

Typical girl, Jake said.

I mean it, she said, put it down.

Check me out, Jake said, and balanced the skull on his head like a bizarre hat.

Guys, stop, I said.

Germs! Emily screeched.

Cool, I'll take a picture, Sam said. He dug in his pocket and pulled a camera out.

Bambi bit the dust, Jake said, and gave a thumbs-up when the flash went off.

I'm serious, Emily said, that's so stupid.

How about this? Sam asked, and he set the skull down and drew back an imaginary bowstring.

Hold that pose, Jake said.

I think we should go, I said.

Relax, Jake said. But they put away the camera and began to climb down. Jake looked a little sorry when he went over to Emily but her pouting wasn't serious and he knew it was all right.

I bet you'd look good in camo, she said.

You okay? Sam asked, approaching, and I nodded, but then he tossed the skull back toward the shore and it crunched on the rocks, not enough to splinter, only roll around a bit before it stopped, eye-up, and suddenly I felt sick.

Around the fire, waiting for the light to drop far enough behind the pine horizon so that we could search for moon-loving crayfish near the shallows, we talked about people we had known once, because what else was there to do when you no longer had school or sports to force you to be friends, and now only met once or twice a year to remind yourself why you kept in touch?

Lora Rivers is pregnant, I said. Emily snorted.

She always was a skank, she said.

You're so mean, Jake said fondly.

Whatever, Emily said. Did you hear about Jenna Murphy?

I think that's supposed to be a secret, I said. I poked the fire and hoped the mosquitoes would land soon so I could go to the tent and listen to them talk about me.

What about her? Sam asked.

How do you know these thing? Jake asked.

She went to rehab last year, Emily said. She leaned forward eagerly.

Her parents don't really want people to know, I said.

Was it alcohol? Jake asked.

Probably worse, Sam said.

She's home now, so it's not really a thing, I said.

I heard it was heroin, Emily said. We all thought about this for a minute and then Sam said, that's sort of serious.

It probably wasn't heroin, I said. Emily shrugged. Jake drew her close to him and put his arm around her and Sam and I watched them from the opposite side of the fire.

You were a little bit of a slut in high school, weren't you? Emily said to me suddenly, and I could tell she was angry that I had disagreed with her before.

No, I said, but Jake whistled and Sam looked at me, and I thought he was smiling, but I couldn't tell in the dim light.

Were too, Emily said.

No, really, I wasn't, I said, and she settled herself a little bit more into Jake and said, sure, and looked away.

No shame, Jake said, maybe kindly, so I shrugged and moved my feet and said, yeah, no shame. Wind moved the leaves and down on the shore the canoes bumped against each other, knocking like hollow snail shells upended on the pebble beach. It was dark now, but I did not want to look for the crayfish anymore.

Have you heard about Paul Stevens' parents? Emily asked. They got divorced because she cheated on him with a coworker.

Rain again. Not heavy like the last time, though, just a sheen that you couldn't exactly see until you passed a hand over your face and your fingers slipped on the water-coated skin that had grown up there in a liquid mask, cool and a little bit oily, water dripping off the end of your nose and poised in strands of droplets in your hair. All around us the lake blurred with mist and we passed through it, skimming on the surface with solemn, slow strokes which left swirling divots that stayed for just a second until the fog closed behind us and they disappeared.

I shared my canoe with Sam and he knelt in the bow with a straight back to keep the rain from pooling over his shoulders. The food pack was pounds lighter by now which meant we sat higher in the water and would tip easier, so when Sam swung around to face me I grabbed for the gunwale with both hands.

Shit, he said, and we both crouched low until the rocking did not carry the lip of the canoe to the waterline.

Why'd you stop? I asked.

Want to look around? he asked.

What about those two? I asked, and he followed the line of my arm toward Emily and Jake, where they had almost reached the portage.

We can meet them at the site later, he said, they know we're following.

I shrugged, and let him take that as a confirmation of sorts. He grinned, and kept at it until I smiled too.

It was a small lake, and shallow, and we let the canoe drift until we wanted to change course with an easy stroke. The rain let off and the water cleared so we could see down to the boulders that loomed out of the dark, ancient glacial teeth brushed once every century by the startled fin of a wide-eyed fish—stones which slept a long sleep down in the cold deep, untouched by any light from above.

It's creepy here, Sam said.

I guess, I said. Something moved in the near forest and the hair on my arms rose, but I clamped my jaw down on the sudden fear and heard nothing more.

It's too late to do it, I said. Two hours of letting the waves direct us among water-lily groves and over drowned trees and we had finally turned to the portage, but now we bumped against a sheer drop-off where the lake ended and the portage trail began and saw that to miss a step, to slip in the dusk, would mean losing supplies and breaking an ankle, and once injured there was nothing to do but wait and hope you'd be found before the food ran out.

You sure? Sam asked.

We're not doing it, I said.

I saw a site sort of back there, he said, and I thought he did not sound nearly sorry enough for having caused this delay.

Emily's going to flip, I said. Sam laughed and the sound was strange in the quiet.

It's not funny, I said, maybe too sharp, because Sam turned his head and said, relax, don't get upset, and even though he smiled at me I did not think he wanted to this time. Wind shook through the pine and birch, and my arms began to ache.

It had been a quick but right decision to split the equipment evenly among the two canoes and so we were not short for food or rope or, highest importance, a tent. Sam struggled with the flysheet and I sat in front of the cook stove and boiled water to the sounds of his impatience, and when the dried peas were plumped into a soggy mess we sat on log stumps and ate.

Do we have anything else? he asked. I tossed him a bag of cranberries.

Eat up, I said, and worked on removing a stuck pea from behind my teeth with my tongue.

Wonder what the other guys are doing right now, Sam said.

I don't think it's hard to imagine, I said.

They're like that? he asked.

I guess, I said. The pea was lodged far back and I tried to dig around with a finger when he glanced away at the brush.

Can't bears, like, smell that sort of thing? he asked, and I yanked my hand from my face.

Myth, I said, and he grinned, said, *nasty*, and with his mouth open I could see cranberry stain on all his teeth, reddish black and thick like blood.

We tied the bear bag with some trouble. There were no good hanging trees and neither of us had much luck catching a branch, toss after toss and the carabiner still dropped at our feet, but in the end we got it up and anchored it with a sapling that we suspected would be bark-stripped come morning where the rope tugged and frayed.

Going to sleep? Sam asked me.

Yeah, I said, you not?

Soon, he said, so I tucked my shoes near the tent flap and crawled in, and when I had tamped down the lumps of earth under the base and moved from side to back to side again and kicked off my sleeping bag and drawn my hood up over my face, I slept.

Footsteps on stone, quiet. I opened my eyes and watched Sam's hand draw the zipper down the tent door, slow, all the way to the bottom before it folded in the material and he crouched in, shoeless and smelling like smoke and sweat. I laid still as he eased the zipper back up, smooth on the sticky spots so it glided up hitchless, so quiet I didn't notice in the dark when he turned around and moved and was close, a sudden shape near my side. I kept my face still and my eyes open and I watched him crawl closer until he stopped, inches away, held a hand near my thigh. In the gray light his hand was white and blue. He put it down and it was warm.

What are you doing? I said. His face was in shadow and I could not see if he was surprised to hear me awake. Nothing was said for a few seconds.

This is what you guys do up here, right? he said.

Sort of, I said.

Outside the tent I could hear the soft scuffles of some quick-pawed creature in the underbrush, noises which went skittering away when Sam put a cautious arm over me and knocked the tent wall.

It's just us, he said, we don't have to say anything about it. He moved his hips over mine and let his weight down gently.

I know that, I said.

It's ok, right? he said.

I don't know, I said. I smelled his breath and he leaned down and then I could taste the berries on his tongue, sweet and hot. He drew back.

Is this ok? he asked. He shifted and I could feel him press against me.

It'll be fine, he said, just us.

It's ok, right? he asked. This is ok?

A loon shrilled out briefly, and then the lake was silent.

It was easy to find Emily and Jake the next morning, and after the site was clear and the bags packed, we loaded up and put in, looking toward fourteen miles that would take us out of the lakes and back into river country, to slow water.

Thanks for letting me get some time with Jake, Emily said from the stern. I concentrated on slicing clean into the waves, perfect angle, and hesitated on each switchover so the drip off the paddle could cool down my knees.

Did you hear me? she asked.

Yeah, I said.

It's nice to get alone time, she said, now that we're pretty serious.

I'm sure it is, I said.

I can't imagine anything better, she said.

I know it, I said, and dug in hard, starting a faster pace. Behind me Emily followed the stroke and we cut through the water with our black shadow stretching far out over the waves, bubbles frothing out from the prow, and we went fast and faster. Blood pumped in my chest and my hands chafed on the paddle, but I did not stop; we shot forward like flint arrows in the pines, or a dog let loose in the night. The stroke ran strong and we went fast over that lake, so that watching from the deep below it was not long before our form passed across the liquid dome—the pale belly of us streaming, luminous—and disappeared.

Wendy Videlock

FEATURED POET

Wendy Videlock

A Moonwalk in a Cowboy Hat: An Interview by David Mason

Wendy Videlock lives in Grand Junction, Colorado, a small city flanked by dramatic mesas where the Colorado River joins the Gunnison River from the south. Known as the Western Slope, and famous for their peaches, Grand Junction and nearby Palisade are also the loci of the state's fledgling wine industry. This is the West as you might imagine it: ranches and farms, and a community that cannot take its cultural life for granted. A visual artist as well as a writer, Videlock is grounded and transported by the place she lives so richly in.

Videlock's first chapbook of poems, *What's That Supposed to Mean,* appeared in 2010 from Exot Books, New York. By then her poems had been appearing regularly in prominent magazines, especially *Poetry,* and would continue to appear in *The Virginia Quarterly Review, The New Criterion, The Poetry Review* (England), and *Quadrant* (Australia), among others. *Nevertheless,* her first full-length collection, came out in 2011 from Able Muse Press and was a finalist for the 2012 Colorado Book Award, followed by *The Dark Gnu,* a book she illustrated, also from Able Muse Press in 2013.

◊ ◊ ◊ ◊

DM: My friend, you and I are westerners, and though I'm older we're pretty much the same generation. For me the West has offered certain silences, the presence of absences, openness, far from the madding crowd—though of course that's changing rapidly, and I'm side-stepping the dark side of the West, the way the cult of individuality has always gotten murderous now and then. I'm thinking the West impresses itself on a poet in different ways than the East does, but I could get lost in generalizations here. I've been away from Colorado all summer, though, in the cooler country of my youth, so tell me how it's been. How have you passed your days on the Western Slope? How's the river? How's the sky? How's the mesa?

WV: They remain good companions. Yes, the west is home—murderous, mysterious, and bent toward consolation. My upcoming book ends on a poem called "El Alma del Oeste" ("The Soul of the West"). The landscape doesn't just seem to inform the work, but actually gives form to the work.

DM: On your blog, *The Fifth Element,* I found the following statement: "It is not possible to possess a love of language without also loving silence." Can you talk about those two loves? Where do they come from? How do they grow?

WV: Yes, silence is underrated and language overused. Where these things come from I can't really say. My love of them probably grew in the dark, and like everything else, had to fight for some sunlight. I think it was Frost who said, "One must be a little secret in order to secrete." This seems to be true of my nature.

DM: Ah, "The secret sits in the middle and knows." So what drove you to write poems in the first place?

WV: I was driven by love, of course. And the money.

DM: And how do you keep the silence in the language?

WV: By making the sounds count, perhaps. That's such a great question. I wish I had a great answer.

DM: That is a great answer. If the sounds count, so will the silences? But there's another way of silence in your work, which does seem to me different from a lot of contemporary poetry. The word "I" is silent, rarely appearing in your poems, which still strike an intimate nerve in readers. How do you see the relationship between writer and reader?

WV: I do not know which to prefer . . .

I'm actually just self-absorbed enough to believe that the pronoun goes without saying. Any observation I make about the world is of course one I've observed in myself; all sorrows and joys depend on love, a good satire doesn't just sink its teeth into the other guy's jugular, etc.

I only know that the relationship between writer and reader is interactive and based on an assumption of distance. So perhaps the relationship is really between distance and intimacy, or the individual and the collective. Maybe that's what writer and reader represent. Any given text is just a place for both to reside, confide, conflict—or drift.

DM: Was there a time in your early work where you relied on the first-person pronoun more? If so, was there ever a conscious decision to work away from its use?

WV: I haven't been conscious of any shift on that in my work. I don't find the "I" off-putting in general. The pronoun is so important, though, isn't it? I often fiddle with pronouns and point of view. I mean, at some juncture, one really struggles with one's own sense of the genuine, and the range therein. There is a world of difference between buying into and believing. I can't muster any interest in the former. Aye would probably Aye more often if my Aye were capable of escaping its limitations.

DM: What can I say but "Aye"? Let me press on these connections a bit more. Distance/intimacy, individual/collective—is art really about transcending these dualisms we use? Can you talk about that in relation to a poem of yours, "If Not for the Dark?"

WV: Ah, if not for the dark, no spark. Consciousness is tricky. We may contain multitudes, but it's easier and often more efficient to perceive things in terms of black and white, right and wrong, up/down, conservative/progressive, etc. I don't know if we can really transcend these perceptions, but art seems to allow us to reside between the poles, giving us a glimpse of what's possible there. The in-betweens, unions and ambiguities seem to flourish in the arts and esoteric systems; perish in commerce and politics.

DM: I'm still thinking of that relationship between writer and reader—who is writing whom and who is reading whom? The whimsical title of your first chapbook *(What's That Supposed to Mean)* plays on that relationship, doesn't it? And plays with social hierarchies and responses. Someone contemptuous of art might ask that question, but it could be asked for a multitude of motives.

WV: So true. Who was it said, you don't read a poem; it reads you . . .

    That said, I think the quest for meaning is a natural one, and I am not one to coolly imply meaning doesn't matter. Now there's a phrase I could spend some time with—Meaning Matters. Can Meaning Matter? The Matter of Meaning. What does Matter Mean? But I *digest*. The problem, or the irony—and the reason I couldn't resist the title—is that by demanding immediate accessibility of a poem, we've already conceded any interest in nuance or reflection, where meaning so often resides.

DM: Yes, and not trusting the reader to work independently. Your poems collude with readers, assume we have the intelligence to engage. I'm thinking about the social world and the private world. That is, I know a kind of tribal life has been important to you, but I also know you can retreat like a hibernating bear. I know your poems can be popular and accessible, and I also know you can play with gnomic riddles. How do you negotiate these insider/outsider realms?

WV: Yes, one would be unbearable without the other. Those insider/outsider realms were more difficult when I was young and felt a need to make excuses for myself when I disappeared. I've learned to make room for my solitude and revel in it.

DM: Perhaps you could comment on "My Moses" here. Who is your Moses and where are you being led?

WV: On the surface, "My Moses" is our beloved mutual friend, Jack Mueller.

> My Moses
>
> Big Jack and his walking stick
> live on the ridge. Kokapelli's
> orphan kids dance for him,
> bobcat urine's in the weeds,
> the shotgun barrel's up his sleeve,
> a Persian coin is on the wind.
> The Chinese Mountains smell the moon
> and arch their backs. I tell him, Jack,
> sometimes I wish I was living in
> canvas France, the old west,
> a picture book, the Sea
> of Tranquility, or even in
> the den near the hot spring.
> He says, kid, to hell with

> phantom limbs; spring is a verb,
> a wish is a wash, a walking stick
> is a gottdam wing.

The conversation never actually happened, of course, but I think the poem touches on something essential about my friendship with him. I'm very drawn to straight-shooters, eccentrics, curmudgeons. I trust them completely. They can be stubborn, difficult, opinionated, pragmatic, but they are never liars. We need more of them in this world. Jack can call me a "formulist", or "ruined by rhyme" and I actually feel complimented. These two characters might be thought of as the elder and the younger, or perhaps the secularist and religionist, the anima and animus, the activist and pacifist. Those crossroads and intersections always interest me. I rather hated to give him the last word in the poem, but one could do worse than end on a gottdam wing.

DM: Good old Jack. Thinking back to our little discourse on the Aye of "I," I fondly remember Jack's heckling poets with "It's not about you." And of course it never is, except as we reside in the "it." Your tribe may be outside the academy, as it were, but its denizens are smart people who keep learning and teaching. What do you read?

WV: I tend to read across genres. I've just finished Roger Shattuck's *Forbidden Knowledge: from Prometheus to Pornography*, which should make me sound awfully racy. I'm currently reading an art history book by Paul Johnson, a book of poetry by Karl Krolow, and a novel by Penelope Lively. Imagine having the name "Lively"—what a gift and a curse that would turn out to be. The passage in the current book that hooked me:

> Our connection with reality is always tenuous. I do not know by what magic a picture appears on my television screen, or how a crystal chip has apparently infinite capacities. I accept, simply. And yet I am by nature skeptical—a questioner, a doubter, an instinctive agnostic. In the frozen stone of the cathedrals of Europe there coexist the Apostles, Christ and Mary, lambs, fish, gryphons, dragons, sea-serpents and the faces of men with leaves for hair. I approve of that liberality of mind.

DM: And what are the great reading experiences of your life?

WV: Most of my peak experiences were when I was young and liberality of mind came easier. When I was thirteen or so, my brother, rolling his eyes at whatever I was reading at the time, handed me a copy of *Thus Spoke Zarathustra*. That pretty much left me changed forever. Not only because it was written with such passion and authority and... madness, but because I found myself both in awe and in philosophical disagreement. So much for liberality of mind. My inner contrarian was probably born that day. I began with some degree of intention to feed my curiosities and interests. Soon after, I started exploring the works of Dostoyevsky, Hesse, Goethe, Camus . . . those guys were intense comrades for a scrappy teen growing up in Tucson. I developed a perverse love of the eloquent and the depressed. As a child I'd been deeply enchanted by faery tale and nursery rhyme, Kipling and de la Mare, and these broody philosophers from cold climes seemed, somehow, a natural progression. It was around that time I discovered Yeats, whose early poem, "The Stolen Child" was pure magic for me—both terrifying and comforting. The imagery in his poems began to enter my dreams at night. Yeats led me to that crazy old bat, Madame Blavatsky, the founder of Theosophy, which, as a belief system, I to this day do not hate. And then there was Millay— specifically "Renascence," and "Love is Not All"—both of which struck me down and lifted me up and made me wish to speak the language of poetry.

DM: Much to respond to here, so I'd like to propose a two-part question—so much seems to be coming in twos! First, I'm struck by your across-genre reading. Many poets refuse to read fiction, as if it would pollute something in them. What, for you, is the particular experience of reading fiction as opposed to nonfiction?

WV: Well, fiction seems to ground me. We rackum schmackum modern lyric poets have forgotten our storytelling roots—but I don't have to tell you that.

DM: No you don't. I'm wondering how fiction and lyric poetry crack open imaginal realms in their different ways. How they remind us of a fuller experience. Can you talk about that?

VW: Well, you just said it—a desire for the whole is probably the thing. If the lyric poem is water, story is the soil.

DM: Lovely! Okay, second part of my original question: I wonder if the Yeats poem you mention, "The Stolen Child," isn't a presiding spirit for your second full-length book, *The Dark Gnu,* which addresses children as well as adults. What's the quality of experience you're after there?

WV: I can't seem to escape Yeats, so it probably did. I wrote the book as my own children were coming of age and leaving the nest, so I was filled with the emotions of change. It was a strange process, putting together that book—addressing children in print made me very self-conscious about interpretation. Ultimately, I hoped the book would embody the spirit of the universal maternal—that is, I wished to deliver a note of both comfort and warning about the world. But it's also very much a funny book, and filled with peculiarities and shenanigans. "Rupert," for instance, is a nod to humor itself as a saving grace, and is also a tribute to my husband.

DM: I like that poem a lot. It begins, "The day that Rupert crossed his eyes/ and cracked an egg/ against his head the people said. . . ." Then we get this list of all the ways people called him crazy. But the outsider is in the know:

> But Rupert didn't say a word,
> but took his daughter by the hand,
> for Rupert knew a thing or two—
> and Rupert knew his little girl
>
> (who had been sad
> for one whole day
> and a half), could likely use
>   a little laugh.

It's not just the delayed information of his motive for comedy, but also wonderful little touches like that half-line "and a half," following like a stumbling afterthought on the line before it. The poem is simple and charming, but partakes of a whole literature of the "wise fool."

    This is what they call "deceptive simplicity," I guess, and it's a quality de la Mare had in his best poems, touching on the mythic sources of our personal stories. I'm thinking of your sonnet called "Who":

> Who
>
> It was the blind girl from the rez who
> stole the baker's missing bread;
> it was the guitar playing fool who crooned
> and raced the wild mustangs through our heads.
> It was the village idiot who played
> his chess without the fool, the bowl
> of soup who said too late, too late, too late
> to blame the thread, the spoon, the text, the mole.
>
> Beside the waterfall of fallen things
> just east of town, it was the bearded man
> attaching fallen things to angel's wings
> while singing legends to the long, long grass.
>
> It was the moon who laughed and laughed.
> It was the moon who laughed herself in half.

There's a quality of improvisation that reminds me of Bob Dylan, riffing on preexisting tropes until they spill some of their secret life. Has music meant as much to you as reading?

WV: I think so. Dylan is another whose influence is inescapable. And elusive. He's a modern-day Hermes, that one. Interesting that you should choose "Who" alongside "Rupert"—both seem to be pointing toward laughter as some kind of force in the universe. And both were inspired by my husband. I think genuine humor is a kind of renewal, a point at which we get to begin again. Auden said that among those he liked or admired, he could find no common denominator; among those he loved he could: they all made him laugh.

DM: The Irish poet Michael Hartnett wrote, "Poets with progress/ Make no peace or pact./ The act of poetry/ is a rebel act." There's a civilizing chiasmus in the way he says it. Do you agree with him? Is the imaginative life a form of rebellion, or is it something else?

WV: It's very Yeatsian. I wish I did agree, because it sounds so awfully good. But I can't go along with the sentiment. The imaginative life probably comes from the same root as what we call the religious impulse. Now that will get me in trouble! I am always wary of holding poetry (or poets), up as something inherently special, courageous, rebellious, angelic, etc. A woman writing poems under a shroud of secrecy in Afghanistan—that's a rebel act.

DM: Indeed. Yet even unheroic poetry can be a form of resistance, not that your problems or mine amount to a hill of beans in this world. Let's try another dramatic question. What are your obsessions?

WV: Good grief, where to begin. I obsess over the right word. The wrong word. A stanza break. The state of the human soul. The state of my own soul. What evolution really means. How theory so quickly turns to belief. The eye of the elephant. The sound of the coyote. The sapling that might not make it through the winter. The source of an old proverb or creation myth. Like most poets, I'm taken by mystery, the sources of things, the underbelly. Observing the way my cat interacts with the world has become a satisfying little obsession. She seems to have a remarkably active inner life, and a very short attention span, which I can rather relate to. I sketch her body's lines, examine the bottoms of her paws, spend hours trying to reproduce the color at the tips of her ears, master the sound she makes when she's mildly annoyed, imagine night vision and its implications, compose theories on what is feral and what is not. That's pretty obsessive. I mean, I could just feed her every morning and scratch her back now and then. Mostly, I'm obsessive about ideas and concepts and systems that have fallen out of fashion. Feeling is mighty fine, and craft is the necessary spine, but abstractions and the imagination aren't exactly chopped liver. I hope never to go in fear of them. Actually, I'm beginning to wonder if these are obsessions or simple distractions . . .

DM: Again I see you resisting truisms. I'm reminded of Stevens talking about the imagination pressing back against the pressure of reality. Is there a "pressure of reality" for you?

WV: Yes, indeed. It is the blight we are born for. And now I'm wondering how Stevens felt about Hopkins. I should know that, shouldn't I?

DM: Why should you know that? Are poets supposed to know everything about other poets? Speaking of other poets, you've been compared to two who tell it slant, particularly those who do it with brevity. You know the ones—Emily Dickinson and Kay Ryan. I don't want to belabor the comparison, but to notice something else. There's a playful, diversionary aspect to much of your work. For example, you called your first full-length book *Nevertheless*, as if it came mid-debate or mid-conversation. Can you talk about that?

WV: Yes, it's a word that's always placed between things, isn't it? And poetry itself is an ongoing conversation, so I like that way of looking at it. Where would we be without adverbs?

The upcoming book is a another kind of slippery tongue. Its tentative title: *Slingshots and Love Plums*. I'm far too easily amused.

DM: That could be a definition of the poet: one who is too easily amused. I'll hang on to that. And the brevity. You've spoken about the short attention span of your cat. Do you start small and build your poems, or do you start large and whittle them down?

WV: The poems come to me small. I have no lung capacity. "The Owl" began as a very long poem, several pages, in fact. I ended up plucking one tiny passage and disregarding the rest. But that was unusual.

DM: Yes, that's a striking little poem:

> Beneath her nest,
> a shrew's head,
> a finch's beak
> and the bones
> of a quail attest

the owl devours
the hour,
and disregards
the rest.

There's something about the way it shifts expectation—devouring the hour rather than the creatures themselves, disregarding rather than digesting or not digesting. I like the toughness of that one, but there's a toughness in a lot of your poems as well as a sweetness. I mean "What Humans Do" is basically a list of euphemisms for fucking, but it's so commandingly ordered in a strong two-beat rhythm and comes, as it were, to such a nice rhyming close, that it climaxes and satisfies. It's affectionate, ultimately:

The candlelit
after-dinner
careful screw,

the under-the-moon
shooby doo
be doo groove,

the from behind,
the sixty-nine,
the is there time,

the I need wine,
the twisted talking
dirty grind,

the Erica Jong
zipless screw,
the I-got-somethin'—

to-prove ruse,
the primal bang,
the power game,

the long play,
the itchy-ish, sudden-ish
roll in the hay,

    the take me away,
    the once a month
    married way,

    the hail mary,
    the holy-joe-
    I-can't-believe-

    my-luck hump,
    the side to side
    slow pump,

    the grudge fuck,
    the quick poke,
    the hard core,

    the tenderest lap
    of waves on the shore,
    and the gushing rushing

    endless coming
    of I've never felt
    this way before.

So I'm thinking about this sweet toughness in your work, the bittersweet of Eros. Is that something you're aware of?

WV: Well, it doesn't sound off to me. I actually only recently read the Anne Carson book.
    "What Humans Do" was written in a matter of moments—one of my most spontaneous poems. Would that they all came like that . . .

DM: That Carson book, *Eros the Bittersweet,* is wonderful. And that poem of yours—a lucky coming. I once gave a joint workshop/reading with you in Colorado, and I remember the magic you worked with an exercise in which students wrote list poems. Where do you get that stuff? Exercises, I mean. Do you use it with yourself as well as in teaching?

WV: Funny, I remember that day as one in which you were the one working the magic.
    I find that in general, both children and adults are pretty suspicious of the subconscious. They want to write, or paint, but they've convinced themselves the process begins on the paper. So I tend to give students exercises which are very simple but also very systematic.

The more they concentrate on the system, the more they seem able to access the imagination or intuitive center. In this way they begin to get the idea that "creativity" has something to do with surprise or discovery, which seems to me rather key. The subconscious doesn't just contain the demons, but also the gold. I don't use these exercises when I'm writing, no, but I do think working in form makes use of the same liberating principle.

DM: Lists. Why are they poetic?

WV: Oddly, I'm compelled to say because they are purposeful.

DM: I know what you mean. But tell me what you mean anyway.

WV: I tend to associate purpose with meaning—or in some vague sense, design, which I believe does govern in a thing so small. I don't ever really know where a poem is going to go or what it wants to do—but something seems to. It's all a great mystery to me. As it happens I've written a little squib on just that subject. It's called "Enjambed":

> It isn't where
> a line ends
>
> or how it begins,
>
> but whether it deems
> itself feigned
>
> or suddenly, strangely
> ordained.

DM: As if the design were just beyond our ken, but present nevertheless. The things we know before we know them, like children grasping at words. How do you feel about poetry in education? What's your experience of how it's done and how it might be done? Your experience as both a teacher and student would come into play here.

WV: I no longer teach in any formal capacity or within the system, and when I did, I taught K-12, so I'm probably not qualified to speak to that. I will say the proliferation of MFA programs doesn't annoy me as it does many of our contemporaries. Greatness—or mediocrity—can come from any background. That said, it wouldn't be a bad idea to move away from the workshop model.

DM: What would that mean, moving away from the workshop model? I've tried it and sometimes find that students get upset when the subject is not themselves. This worries me.

WV: Yes, well, there you have it. We are living in a selfie world. On how best to educate at the college level, I have more questions than answers, I'm afraid. I'd rather pick your brain on that . . .

DM: My brain was plucked long ago. We're rounding a bend here and I can see something ahead. Let me ask this: Are you ambitious?

WV: I'm not driven by a need for recognition or success, but I do feel a need to send the work into the world, and I like to believe I'm writing for my life—which is my idea of playing for mortal stakes. I think there is a kind of ambition in perfectionism, and I certainly have that.

DM: What would you like to achieve?

WV: I'd like to walk on the moon. In a cowboy hat.

DM: And while still earthbound, I'd like to know whether you've ever read any how-to books on writing poetry, or on prosody, and what you make of them.

WV: I've read, or skimmed, many over the years. They are necessary beasts. When they're good they're very good; when they're bad they're horrid. I often recommend *The Rule that Liberates* (Richard Moore), and *The Cure of Poetry in an Age of Prose* (Mary Kinzie), and of course *All The Fun's In How You Say A Thing* (Timothy Steele). I often use ideas from *How Does a Poem Mean?* (Ciardi) when I teach, in large part because I adore the title. And I couldn't help enjoying Stephen Fry's *The Ode Less Travelled*. Ah, and one more: Alfred Corn's *The Poem's Heartbeat*.

DM: That's a good list of books. It's a strange genre. Who knew that even something so unremunerative as poetry could produce legions of followers. It's good to be reminded that in all the chatter about poetry there are graceful and engaging voices to be found.
    Let me move on to something else. A while ago I asked you about the influence of music on your work, thinking of lyricists like Dylan, among other things. I've avoided asking you something far more obvious. You're a painter, and a very particular kind of painter with an unusual palette. *The Dark Gnu* is a book of paintings as well as poems. How did you come to painting? Can you tell us about the particular technique you practice—is

it as laborious as Blake's infernal method, for example? And how do painting and poetry inform each other or play with each other, as the case may be?

WV: I'm a hopeless dabbler. Painting is another way for me to break from language that I might return to it. I can paint with music blaring and with distractions about—when writing I must have total silence. But they are similar in that the process for both is often laborious, sometimes spontaneous, and usually a mixture of both. In both mediums I find myself spilling forth a kind of atmosphere in order that I might discover detail. Or perhaps what I mean to say is that I surrender to something random in order to touch on what feels (for lack of a better word) destined or necessary. That sounds awfully esoteric, doesn't it? So be it! It's all a great mystery to me.

DM: Then we'll end on a note of mystery. Thank you, Wendy.

WV: Thank you, Dave. It's been a pleasure.

★ ★ ★

Works by Wendy Videlock Cited

"Rupert" is from *The Dark Gnu and Other Poems* (Able Muse Press, 2013)

"The Owl," "My Moses," "Who," "What Humans Do," and "Enjambed" are from *Nevertheless* (Able Muse Press, 2011); "Enjambed" first appeared in *Quadrant,* and the others in *Poetry.*

FEATURED POETRY
NEW POEMS FROM WENDY VIDELOCK
★ ★ ★

Wendy Videlock

These Are the Things I Think I Know:

There's nothing whiter than the snow.
If it isn't a bridge it's a puppet show.
There are single cells which intertwine.
There are yogis who have lost their minds.
You are not you. You are not a twin.
Not every horse makes the medicine.
There are towers that have no sense of time.
There are poets who will not scan a line.
The end will place its bets on the start.
Beware the ram without an art.
The visions that will not meet the eye
will loom to remind you that you're blind.
The breeze that changes everything
will never stop to leave her name.
There are words that do not coincide.
There are students who cannot cross the divide.
The albatross that you must bear
will rob from the soul and give to the air.
Each poverty and heartache knows
the size of the kernel left in the bowl,
what to smash, and what to hone,
the golden rib, and the goldilocks zone.

Wendy Videlock

The Vigilantes

The vigilantes. They're the ones
who look you in the eye and say
it takes a year of warm and cold
to string a house with twinkle lights,
to know the tiger from the corn,
to see the face within the stone
or taking shape within the clouds
is probably your own. The place
the vigilantes vanish in
is paper thin, and flecked with gold.
They sleep inside the triangle
which opens just before it folds.
Or falls, like snow. It's they who turn
the leaves to burnished bits of light.
They speak of wheat, but secretly.
The vigilantes stir the roots
of thunder trees, and underneath,
an ocean springs. Their storms will form
a shore where words escape their lips
to brutalize us with tenderness—
their pale gray afternoon eyes
trailing away like mayflies.

Wendy Videlock

Invocation

The scent, the chase, the wound, the rain—
here lies
the sandhill crane that I became—

I, Coyote,
most at home on the road
     possess the ghosts

of Hermes and of Crazy Horse,
of spotted fish and figure eights,
      of damselfly

and coral snake—

the shifting shape which slithers in
to break apart
your theories and your stoic heart

is never home
    is always home
is most at home where a gathering storm
    and a whale bone
  upturn

a wisp of smoke
     and a stepping stone.

Wendy Videlock

What the Sculptor Said

Given a whit of vision and precision,
a man can chip away at a thing,
revealing the shape that lies within:

    Pallas Athena,

The Thinker, The Kiss,

      The Griffin's Wing.

Given this inexplicable itch
to know the shape that lies within
(by chipping and chipping away at a thing),

    it's wise to recall

this can also result

      in nothing at all.

Wendy Videlock

In the Wind

In the wind, by the lake,
a friend
turns around to say,
just so you know,

the wind carries your words away.

Anthony Mastroianni
Midnight in Paris

My leg hurts. My balls ache. My head feels ten times heavier than it should. I feel like a gaping asshole and, well, she, she's perfect.

You know that girl who's the perfect height with or without heels on? Her wrong opinions are right. She hasn't seen *Everybody Says I Love You* because she doesn't like musicals. Even her ugly fucking haircut looks great. She doesn't even like *Midnight in Paris,* but all she's doing is midnight in Paris-ing your ass and you're getting further and further lost in this paradox called Annamari'.

She's that girl you don't address directly so it seems like you are talking to everyone, but you're only responding to the shit she says. She's in your head and in that head you are the only two people at the table even though your girl is on your arm and has been the whole night. You're surrounded by friends and acquaintances, but they aren't *there* there. They're background noise. "Dream Weaver" is playing. She's that girl.

Next thing you know, party's over. The CD is skipping and you snap out of it. Your friends and friends' friends are in the forefront again. You bid farewells and kiss cheeks. You save the best for last. Your real girl is on the other side of the terrace trying to organize cab rides with someone else, but *she* is right in front of you.

You have been waiting all night for this. It's straight up nothingness. It's the same kiss on the cheek you shared with Pasquale and Cinzia and like a hundred other Antonios, the same kiss on the cheek you gave your mom when you said goodbye and to her it will be just that. Nothing. You look at the floor between you and glance up every couple of seconds. Scruples. You hope the cigarette you've just stuffed in your mouth hides the fact that breathing any deeper would look like an asthma attack.

Now she's looking at the floor too. You're scared she's probably searching the tiles for whatever is scaring the bejesus out of you.

You don't even have the chance to stop another second and admire those black ass eyeballs or all those muscles in her face reaching upward to grab a hold of her super cheekbones, all that stuff that's working together to form that forever shit-eating grin, when she reminds you how much she likes the green paint on your shoes. She's like that. She likes that you've got green paint on your shoes and maybe she is the most beautiful girl you've ever seen.

All you manage to say is that you like her shoes too. Something-something white shoes are dope.

This is where you should have jumped off the terrace.

In fact, this is exactly where you should have jumped off the terrace, but she looks straight into your eyes, straighter than any straight shit ever. It's not the same way you lock eyes before a first kiss. There is no instinctual move. You just freeze. You freeze up worse than the ole "I like your shoes back" move and all you want to do is Alex Mac this joint, but she saves you. All casual, smirk, forever shit-eating grin, she goes, "You have green paint on yours. That's blood on mine."

It's not a cool sentence. It isn't romantic. It's the opposite, but they're words directed at you. You tell yourself you just fell in love then and there, as if you hadn't been telling yourself that for about a year and a half.

It could be period blood for all you know. Perhaps she straight up gouged the eyeballs out of the last guy who looked at her the way you're looking at her right now. It's probably a paper cut or something, but who knows

with the way she's got that voodoo shit on you. It's something.

You fall in love too easy.

★★★

Your roommate pats you on the back. The cabs are outside. You forgot where you were. You're in Rione Sanità. Naples. This is Gennaro. He's your roommate. You acknowledge him, whoever he is, blink, breathe through your nose, who knows where your cigarette went. *Chissà chissà, chissà.* By the time you process this stupid emotion, which is immediately, she's disappeared.

You thank your lovely host and say goodbye to your girl who is getting in a different cab, but your eyes are still dragging the lake for this bitch. You just want a goodbye kiss, on the cheek that is, and your roommate directs this asshole driver whose jumping off point is eight euros all the way home. Like he doesn't know where Piazza Plebiscito is. Bozo.

Enter Casa Cupiello.

Your roommate and his girlfriend are beautiful. They are in love. They are in love and they function on the most sane level of being in love. Every gesture one of them makes complements the other. They sit down on the cot in the extra room and chatter. They need no words, but they chatter while you grab a bottle of grappa from under your bed. You offer them each a glass and they decline and thank you while you fill your glass with a copious ass amount and you talk on about the evening. Typical shit. She's so crazy. He's so funny. That apartment is amazing. You try to bring her up the whole time, but you lack the tact to insert her name in a subtle way. You're already blushing. It would be all forced and there would be this look on your face. Better if you don't.

Before you know it they're smiling at you, almost looking at you in pity, goodnighting you, hand in hand, like you should be with her, her—your real girl. Instead you're alone on the couch at three a.m. You must be lonely. Grappa in one hand, some of your hair in the other, staring at the bay, at a volcano, a real volcano and you slip into one of those daydreams even though it hasn't been daytime for a while and there's still a way to go before the next one.

★ ★ ★

Sunday morning and the first clear sky you can remember in weeks. The perfect time for a stroll, a half stroll down the half stroll of our lives. The stairs down to Santa Lucia are bustling like the very image you have of them on a dreamlike day. Ah, Santa Lucia, if you could only see. Buckets full of coins are being lowered from windows and raised full of vegetables and household items. Wives and future wives, widows, are hanging clothes out from their balconies and from one building across the street to another. The alleyways referred to as streets smell like fresh laundry.

Then there's Lungomare. It's as beautiful as ever. People are singing. Little kids are falling down on roller skates. And grownups. You walk on the sidewalk to avoid cyclists or accidentally participating in a street clown's show in the middle of the *via*. You walk and walk until you get to the end of the pedestrian zone where Villa Comunale starts and where you stop and sit on the ledge and watch the sea move under the sun. It's postcard shit. You'll never think of the Sound or the East River as water again. It's a straight nautical experience.

The fishermen are down on the rocks below the ledge. They are doing the same things as you. They're sweating, waiting for something that will probably never come. You sit there watching them, waiting, watching them wait as if one might reel in Parthenope herself. Hemingway used to do this on the Seine, you tell yourself.

"This isn't Paris and you're not Hemingway."

She's sitting next to you like she was there the whole time, like she's been present in your everything. The only person under this sun in all black, reading your mind, that smirk, being your all-around dream girl. You're not gonna question it.

"Naples is my Paris," you tell her with the same twisted-up half a smile she's wearing.

She half giggles (which she pronounces as *jiggles*) and she punches your arm.

In that same half duckface, she points to the direction you came from. Even the way her pointer finger curves upward a little makes your heart beat.

"I'm going that way if you want to walk a little with me."

Of course you'll just take a walk. It's totally innocent—it's a walk! you tell yourself. A walk! It's innocent. You already have a girl and she's great to you. She's giddy *(jiddy)* at the sight of you. She enjoys scratching your head. This girl reads books you like just so she can talk to you about them. She straight admires you. This homegirl would probably do anything for you and so this is just an innocent thing, a walk with a human you know.

You go, "I could use some exercise," and she smiles at you and you return the favor. Imagine spending an entire march along the sea talking about the Marx Brothers and R. Kelly. She says all the right stuff and you can feel people looking at you in envy while you laugh and smile. No one tries to sell you toys or lighters. Not a single rose salesman approaches.

You get to the end of the pedestrian zone, in front of the Castel dell'Ovo. You're ready to say goodbye. Any further turns back into your hood and maybe you want to take the fantasy home with you even more than you do the object of it. You're both looking at your shoes almost toe to toe. The goodbye that never comes. Your eyes follow hers up from your all green Adidas and meet somewhere in that little bit of space that is always between you. It's that little bit of space that implies the little stage direction for the pause and the deeper breathing. *(pause) (deep breathing)*. She breaks it like she always does and turns to the castle.

She's dropping castle history on you. You pretend not to know it all. She looks genuine and happy and proud to tell you and you're happy to listen. It's going on a thousand years old. Word on the street was Virgil put a magic egg under the foundation before it was built and if the egg ever cracks the castle will do the same or something.

The whole city is supposed to crumble. The mythology is great, but most important, it's the only major, historic and non-historically cool monument with free entry.

So conversation leads back to the Marx Bros. and you are gravitating toward the magic egg. Maybe Virgil is guiding you, but it's probably just her. Amidst all your cute jokes (all you need is *l'ovo*) you find yourself atop of Castel dell'Ovo. The air is the freshest. The bay is all sparkling. Every cliché in the book. There's a fucking volcano to your left. A real volcano. You tell her that you like to imagine that if Capri wasn't there you could see straight to New York and she asks if she can give you a kiss on the cheek. Since it's totally innocent, just two people on top of a castle looking out across the clear blue sea and a kiss on the cheek is just a salutation and she is smiling all nervous like a little girl who spun the bottle and the bottle is pointing right at her secret crush and you are just a little schoolgirl's reflection of her yourself and you wouldn't want to be the one to kill that feeling, would you? And it's only a common salutation. Before you can scream SÌ, SÌ, SÌ! she plants one on the side of your face and backs away with the same nervous face and surprised speed that she came in with. You reciprocate the same. You are staring at each other with that "I'm in love with you" face when you snap the fuck out of it.

Your phone is ringing.

You ignore it. It's probably just your girl calling to say, "Goodnight Marcello," and tell you what a great time she had with you tonight. You can just send her a message in the morning that says you were already sleeping and that *you* had such a good time with *her* last night.

You try to slip back into the fantasy, but it's forced. It's just you and Annamari' standing, looking at a bunch of water.

You check your watch that your girl surprised you with after you pointed it out that time at the swap meet by the giant ugly post office building with the fascist architecture. It's going on four. But maybe you should call her back though. You gulp down the rest of your cup which is or isn't a lot depending on where you're at and try to stand up which is or isn't a lot depending on where you're at. You take one step and fall over the arm of the couch.

You're lying there on the floor. The dream is gone. The only thing you can think is, my leg hurts, my balls are aching, my head weighs more than the rest of me and maybe she's perfect.

Robert W. Crawford

Calypso Calls on Penelope

Did you buy that load of crap? The bit
about his need to be a handyman,
the touching speech on being "home"—bullshit.
I'm here to tell you why he really ran.
He says he's back to fix what needs repair.
Truth, dear, he couldn't keep up with the sex—
outrageous games, immortal underwear,
positions that required him to flex.
Blah, blah, he made that bed, he wants to care;
fact is, he's slowing down, he's often tired—
you've noticed that he's started losing hair,
how more and more he fails to get inspired?
Penelope, honey, you ought to know:
he didn't want to leave, I made him go.

Duane Caylor

Cicero Comments

1. On Searching Syracuse for Archimedes' Tomb

Through streets as narrow as a Gallic mind,
I wandered through the city and inquired
of every ancient Greek where I could find
the mausoleum where they had interred
that architect and fulcrum of their fame:
old Archimedes who, in reverie,
was slain by my coarse countryman who came
and proved a point with trigonometry
disguised as steel. At last, I found his tomb
wrapped in a shroud of brambles, briars, and weeds,
the laurels of obscurity or blame
rather than fit memorial to great deeds.
And so I learned there is no ratio
inscribing genius in an afterglow.

2. On the Pleasures of the Garden

Here in converging twilights, let me rest.
While day ebbs slowly westward out to sea
and gathers hope with which it will invest
tomorrow's dawn, may heaven's tranquility
fall with the shadows from the myrtle bough,
stretched like beatitude above my head,
as Zeno and his brothers tell me how
to persevere these dark hours without dread.
The scents of mint, bay, cypress, oleander,
and rose still waft through this gymnasium
despite aspirants after Alexander
who've taken Rome in turn. In Tusculum,
the sunsets and the gardens are so fine
we almost doubt republican decline.

3. On Writing His *Cato the Elder*

The skill it takes to make a specious claim
wrapped in the toga of an ancient's words
to cloak its incredulity with fame
shows rhetoric both skillful and absurd.
Such argument is best if not profound
or tightly logical, but rather flows
digressively in order that the sound
of language drape what logic would disclose.
I hoped in writing *De Senectute*
to cure the fear of death that all contract,
treating with Xenophon's philosophy
of golden-laureled age to come. In fact,
if winter really looked so good from fall,
there would have been no need to write at all.

4. His Last Oration

I see them coming down the path like hounds
invigorated by the scent of prey.
I've struggled to escape, and made the rounds
from shore to ship to shore, but cannot stay
this game's end any longer. Put the litter
under that knobby pine where I can wait
for death in peaceful shade. I would not fritter
this final time away in vain debate.
Young Caesar cast me out into this dark
new world where dogs that pant for Anthony
pursue, and now so close I hear them bark.
I'll meet them here. You, soldier! Look to me!
To kill a senator, as if a stoat,
is base! But do it well. Here is my throat.

ABLE MUSE WRITE PRIZE FOR POETRY, 2014 ▪ FINALIST

Catherine Chandler

Discovery

The Cassette

Emptying your scented dresser drawers,
I came across an old cassette you'd hidden
(back then clairvoyant readings were forbidden).
Worn weary by the grind of humdrum chores,
you'd sent a snake-oil quack a bobby pin—
and who knows how much cash—so he could see
what was, what is and what would surely be,
lending your life a favorable spin.

You must have sat there sneering at the fraud,
as I do now, through sixty minutes of
his slippery bunkum vouching for your love
of family, country, gardening and God.
I'll never know now, Mother, if he guessed
those few things right, and misconstrued the rest.

What You Kept

A mildewed trunk defending old receipts,
a cookie tin,
discolored carpets, pillowcases, sheets.
Easy enough, as are the Mason jars,
stuff for the trash or the recycling bin,
the church bazaars.
I toss aside what's always needled me—
the plaque from John Paul's Holy Jubilee,

the Norman Rockwell mugs, the Kinkade prints.
From underneath
a roll of batting and a bolt of chintz
I pull a faded ribbon-festooned box.
Inside, my fairy-stolen baby teeth
and first shorn locks
acknowledge, in an elegant goodbye,
that I was once the apple of your eye.

Anne-Marie Thompson

Sonnet

The blizzard thick, the wind-shrieks closing in,
the evening sky battered and blistered white
as childhood scars, two lovers, safe within
their blanket-bundled noon, deflect the night
and all its chaos to an infinite hush,
each clinging to the other as the mind
clings to a flake of heaven that would rush
away at day and leave no dream behind.
They cannot hear the madness or the bare,
raging finality of silent space,
so deafened are their ears to all the air
except their own sparked whispers, which they trace
with snow-lit fingernail in place of pen,
leaving these flurried letters on their skin.

BOOK REVIEW

Martin McGovern
Three Reviews:

Stephen Kampa, *Bachelor Pad*
The Waywiser Press, 2014
ISBN 978-1-904130-58-1, 104 pp., UK £8.99, paperback

Quincy R. Lehr, *Heimat: A Poem*
Barefoot Muse Press, 2014
ISBN 978-1-4996-3456-3, 78 pp., USA $10.95, paperback

Joshua Mehigan, *Accepting the Disaster*
Farrar, Straus and Giroux, 2014
ISBN 978-0-374-10098-8, 96 pp., USA $23.00, hardcover

★ ★ ★

"Who would have thought there'd be so much variety here?" one might ask (echoing Lady Macbeth, of course) after reading these three exhilaratingly different volumes of mainly formal poetry. Or, I guess one just can't slap the categorical term "formal" poetry on all three of these books: they each use form in, thankfully, their own distinct ways, and the poets are as adept at writing free verse as they are at formal poems. The reader, however, might just come away from the three books, books strongly based in form, with some very different kinds of head shaking and some exuberant head nodding.

Joshua Mehigan's *Accepting the Disaster* is the most straightforward collection of this trio, and Mehigan himself, judging from his bio and his previous collection of poems—*The Optimist* (Ohio University Press), which was a finalist for the 2005 *Los Angeles Times* Book Prize in Poetry and winner of the Hollis Summers Poetry Prize—is probably the most straightforward poet in terms of, you know, the standard "career poet," in the maybe old-fashioned academic way: he's gone through his enviable sequence of individual publications in the tried and the true—*The New Republic, The New York Times, The New Yorker, The Paris Review,* and *Poetry*. And he is a teaching fellow at the College of Staten Island and a workshop instructor for Brooklyn Poets. (And, yes, he has lived in NYC, for the past 20 years.)

Accepting the Disaster's poems are pretty darn straightforward, too. They have a metrical and rhyme solidity that, while not heavy-handedly boxing one's ears, certainly make an announcement that that is what the reader is in for, rhyme (mostly full-on rhyme) and meter, mostly full-on iambic/anapestic/trochaic meter) beginning with the book's first stanza:

> Nothing has changed. They have a welcome sign,
> a hill with cows and a white house on top,
> a mall and grocery store where people shop,
> a diner where some people go to dine.
>
> — "Here"

The simplicity of diction and the directness of statement and rhyme are, by my lights anyway, appealing. The poet is willing to move slowly, to look at things as they come to him, and not run willy-nilly all over the town trying to find out what the town is about. This simplicity is a simplicity of diction and rhyme and, really, a way of looking one finds in early Snodgrass, especially the wonderful *Heart's Needle,* where that poet takes us calmly but sternly and clearly (as clearly as his mind and heart will let him) on a journey of self-discovery, a discovery of who he, W.D. Snodgrass, is and how he came to be who he is.

But there is a departure from Snodgrass's style (and, I'd say, from his way of looking at the world), and it can be located in the sense one gets reading *Disaster* that Mehigan is out to teach *us* something. Whether it is something like we learn at the end of the opening poem, "Here" ("Nothing here ever changes, till it does"), or what we are told at the end of "Down in the Valley": "Nature is just. There's nothing left to fear/ The worst thing that can happen happened here." Mehigan is, not to be too cranky about it, full of lessons, as one might say the subject of one of Mehigan's poems, "Father Birmingham," might have been: "He's an important part of who I am./ He taught me not to be but to behave."

Don't get me wrong, I'm all for learning lessons from poems about who I am and who I am meant to be. But sometimes with Mehigan's perfect rhyme, or perfect off-rhyme, at the perfect end of the poem to teach me whatever it is I'm being taught . . . well, sometimes I get weary. I'm reminded of rabid followers of Yvor Winters (many of whom were

Stegner Fellows out at Stanford many moons ago): poetry, accordingly, was something of a regime to help make one a better person. Poetry is for bracing us. At least that's how I read certain interpretations of Winters. Poetry can indeed brace us, but it also graces us. It lets us breathe, not standing always at attention, saluting.

Mehigan is fantastic for summing up, as he does in the poem entitled "The Library."

> We have all been there once. Some, more than that.
> They forced us all to visit one September
> But that was such a long, long time ago.
> There wasn't anything to marvel at.
> The door was heavy. That I still remember.
> Inside were many things I'll never know.

This short poem has punch. It has nostalgia: we are quickly taken back to a library in the past, some library, someone's library. And we are told, I guess one could say, what we learn through this experience. All I can say, though, is, "Ya know, this ain't *my* library."

★ ★ ★

If Mehigan comes off as a kind and concerned but somewhat stern father reminding us that there are disasters and that we become who we are by, somehow, accepting them, or at least not letting them put us under, Quincy R. Lehr is very quick to point out, in *Heimat* (a word, an opening note mentions, that in German means "homeland," though "with broader cultural connotations than the English word"), that very many things in life are disasters, and life itself may be a disaster, but at least we can rail against disaster. In fact, life's a mess: people and things (history, for one) are always getting in the way and going awry; the wrong people win; the right people lose. Life, my friends, is . . . well, not really boring, but more than aggravating. And Quincy Lehr is going to rant about it—loud and long and sometimes in pretty amusing ways. But rant he will, using rhyme as a kind of *invention* to keep the rant going.

In contrast to Mehigan's methodical weighing of things past and present, Lehr is off to the races from the very beginning, his prefatory poem, "This Is . . ." rattling the reader awake with:

> This is May and June 2009
> This is five years of my life.
> This is 2,500 years of human history.
> This is coffee and pills and cigarettes and other bad habits and
>   a mind that wasn't on a woman. Really, it wasn't.

And the opening poem turns its ending with the following pronouncement:

> This is the Grand Statement.
> This is the moment where before flipped over to after.
> This is out of chronological order.
> This is the crescendo.
> This is the raised middle finger.
> This is my national epic beating up your national epic.
> This is the big time baby.

So . . . a reader's got to feel he or she is in for a ride, I'd say—maybe the ride of one's life. The exuberance of the introductory poem . . . I don't know, I'm thinking if I say to the poet, "Really? This is it, baby?" I'll get a stink-eyed look and the middle finger.

But Lehr is smarter than that, by a long shot. Born in Oklahoma, Lehr writhes with his freedom of living in New York and teaching history. The author of *Across the Grid of Streets* 2008), *Obscure Classics of English Progressive Rock* (2012), and *Shadows and Gifts* (2013), Lehr apparently writes hard and fast, so fast, in fact, his acknowledgements in this book fly by with an "All of you who pitched in with suggestions, moral support, and the occasional glass of wine know who you are, and you are tops."

What they pitched in on, and what Lehr's cover and back blurbs maintain that this is, is Lehr's *Waste Land* for the present moment. And one has to admire Lehr leading us in the history of Lehr's beginnings in, maybe, Dingle or maybe in Oklahoma City, or the echoes of his beginnings, and back to the beginnings of this very country, and the movement forward, and back to the beginnings of Manhattan and D.C. and their fallings and risings and stumblings to the present. Lehr seems not only to be aiming at, poetically, Eliot but Whitman, too: Tiresias presents himself, as Eliot might have him do, but so do "Bed-Stuy" (Bedford-Stuyvesant), Emerson, Bismarck, the Battle of Resaca, the Communist League, Blake's "New Jerusalem," NYC poverty, and at least one line from "The Battle Hymn of the Republic," many of these explained in Lehr's somewhat Eliotian notes at the back of the book—some of which are helpful for reading the poem, some just extraneous or at least distrustful of the reader's own knowledge.

The poem itself consists of stanzas of varying lengths held together by a weave of ingenious rhymes and off-rhymes. Often, Lehr is impossible to resist, as in the following riff on Tiresias:

> That jerk Tiresias is now asleep
> and snores so loudly that it wakes the neighbors
> who shout out curses. "Keep it down, you creep,
> or medicate! Do yourself a favor!"
> The prophet, though, is out of it and dreaming,
> oblivious to us, and to our scheming.

This is playful poetry, smart poetry, that gives every appearance that it's got a big point to make, or if not one big point, a lot of small necessary ones. I'm no dope, I tell myself (maybe too often), and I grabbed hold of this book with enthusiasm and read it through . . . thrice. The big point? I hate to say it, but I'm not sure. What I take away from *Heimat* is that *this,* whether *this* be a state of mind or a state of the United States, this *homeland* is surely not heaven, that history and what history has brought us to are powerful and have done some powerfully bad things (we, of course, being makers of history and doers of powerfully bad things). If, though, we are willing to give it (history/the present) the middle finger and to knock the snot out of it, then and only then can we call this homeland, this *Heimat,* wherever it may be, home.

★ ★ ★

If Mehigan coaches us to accept disaster and Lehr taunts us to flip it off, Stephen Kampa revels in the simple experience of trying to figure out if living really equates with disaster, if we can "deal with it" if it is disaster, and how might we live with it if it isn't—if life is, in fact, the opposite of disaster. Kampa is authentically exploratory and energetically invites the reader to join him on his artistic and philosophical explorations.

And I'd readily advise the reader to join him—if said reader can get over the unfortunate title of the book, *Bachelor Pad*. (I put off reading this volume, of these three, until last because of the title, but I recommend it, now, first.) I've lived in bachelor pads, though it's been a while. Many of us have, and even if we haven't I think we have some idea of them: the rancid sweat socks stuffed between couch cushions, the overflowing ashtrays, Budweiser empties and a half-filled Jameson bottle, and maybe a condom package or three. Kampa's poetry brushes with this image, but the poems are really much more and much more representative of a young man's search for true meaning in his life, the lives of those around him, and the life of the very world in which he lives. And Kampa does all this with an enviably sure hand at poetic forms and styles.

Kampa refuses to dismiss the dismal and dark hours of our lives. In "Wake," he tells us:

> Here are the random couples bumping uglies,
>   And here, prayer circles squeezing hands;
> Here are the children curled up in their snugglies,
>   And here, tuxedoed bands
>
> Are sweating through their set-to-end-all sets
>   Now that the news of the tsunami
> Has been confirmed. God's sent us his regrets
>   As global origami—

Kampa cannot erase the dream at the end of the poem that has God "pulling that huge blue sheet/ Over the world's face." But the poet is quick, in the next poem in fact, to remind the reader that at "other times, you manage to forget/ The small atrocities, the ambient spite/ That still can overwhelm you . . ." Kampa is unafraid of broaching couples (and couplets), two by two, and the joys and spats that are part of the normal swirl of love and heartache—the reading of Kampa's facility with poetic technique and felicity of style making the immediate world a better place despite the pain of misunderstanding:

> The classic movie channel sometimes plays a pair
> Of films the same leads starred in (Rogers and Astaire,
> Flynn and de Havilland), so musicals might morph
> To hardboiled noir—fedora'd gunmen guard a wharf
> And punctuate the mist with pulsing cigarettes—

While we, as a couple, might enjoy watching noir couples do their thing, Kampa wisely—for a denizen of a bachelor pad—digs deep and finds solace in at least knowing that his night, the night belonging to the couple that he might belong to, may not end the way he wants, but even in knowing that, he's better off than ending up in ignorance:

> . . . what troubled creatures
> We are, who now suspect each other's double features
> And let our programs (onetime classics rereleased
> For TV) do our talking for us, framed in black
> And white. Most nights we take our cues from them, not least
> In how we sleep: for twice as long and back to back.
>
> — "Double Features"

Kampa uses as the book's epigraph a selection from Milton's "Tetrachordon" concerning God's giving Adam an Eve. This is telling not only, of course, in the "bachelor" represented in *Bachelor Pad* and that bachelor's meditations on and experiences with significant others, but also in how Kampa sees the world as a sort of "coupling," whether that be a coupling of sexes (of whatever gender) or a coupling of thought and experience, or a coupling of non-art and art—whether film or music, television or poetry, and all their accoutrements, including actors and directors, audiences, readers, sets and scenes, entrances and exits, dreams and realities. And Kampa has a tangible knowledge, apparently, of many of these:

> I could dissect each frame . . .
> But let's talk outtakes. The clip I have in mind
> Stalls in the locker room: the cops take aim,
> Fire off their lines, and every time, that spritz
> Of deodorant across one's chest (aligned
> > Just so to douse both pits
>
> > In one long arc) reduces
> Them both to fits of giggles. It takes six takes . . .
>
> > — "Outtakes (Three Takes)"

For Kampa, there is joy in art, and joy and pain in the making of it. Just like life, in however many takes it takes. And his pad, his *Bachelor Pad* is a tour de force. Run. Get it. Read it. Live.

ESSAY

Derek Furr
Our Elizabeth, Walcott Mine

At two recent celebrations of the work of Derek Walcott and Elizabeth Bishop, I was surprised, even a little embarrassed, by the public display of affection for our poets. I use "our" here advisedly. She is ours, it was said. He speaks to me. I shouldn't have been so stuffy. At a celebration, expressions of affection are common. Even during the most formal of campus poetry readings, a young admirer will preface his elaborate question to the poet with heartfelt praise of her work. But at these events, there was an urge to claim kinship, that "Bishop lived next door," and "Walcott is an islander like me." These were not so much testimonies to a poet's universality as to her being radically local—rooted, as the adverb suggests, in the land of her readers, all the more so when the poets in question speak eloquently of uprootedness and disorientation. Despite their having become associated with official verse culture inside academia, Bishop and Walcott were, for these readers, beloved poets-in-residence of borderlands and out-of-the-way spaces.

I attended the Walcott event on a rainy November evening in Victoria, BC, the site of an annual conference for humanities scholars. Vancouver Island is a far cry from the Caribbean that provides the landscape and language of Walcott's poetry, and the city was a strange space in which to find him. Warmly nostalgic for the British Empire, downtown Victoria wears its epaulettes and ostrich feathers unabashedly for the sake of tourists and a sense of Commonwealth self. That, at least, is the admittedly limited impression I got as one of those tourists, staying in the conference headquarters at the city's signature hotel, The Empress. I met no one at the conference who didn't attempt to register her self-consciousness about the setting as soon as she introduced herself, making a clever remark about all the Union Jacks, the photos of royalty on elephants (Indian and African), the tea rooms. But there we were, hypocrite readers in a luxury hotel, pampered and comfortable in our discomfort. In the long shadow of the Raj, we were spending liberally despite the recession, declaiming radicalism in the Bengal Lounge, then laughing ironically at ourselves.

Walcott was not in Victoria for the conference but for the Pacific Festival of the Book. He read at the opening of a co-op that could have been The Empress' doppelgänger, her poor lost twin. It had tea but not high tea. It had no peacocks or tusks, no Persian rugs, no floral wallpaper—for that matter, it had no defining aesthetic. Its mission, unlike the Empire's, was ambiguous. Judging from the proprietor's enthusiastic welcoming remarks, the co-op was a local visual arts gallery, fair-trade tea and coffee house, healthy lifestyles seminar space, Bohemian clothing consignment shop and community center. That is to say, it was a Utopian enterprise founded by a poet, not a businessman or politician. For all its confusion, it rivaled, maybe even surpassed, The Empress in its sincerity, something on the order of Linus' pumpkin patch or Donna Reed's family room.

Walcott's audience was as eclectic as the co-op, and several people spoke before the poet began his reading. Over the clatter of flatware and the burbling of coffeemakers, one particularly impassioned fan declared the kinship of all islanders, Vancouver Island being somehow a far northern cousin to Walcott's St. Lucia. In front of me, an elderly woman asked her husband, "Is that the poet?", her whisper the kind that needs no amplification to resonate around a room. A young man, soaked from the rain, dripped by the doorway. He was evidently indifferent to his own discomfort, his eyes glued on Walcott, his hands trembling with excitement rather than the chill. In the midst of it all, Walcott sat serenely, his thick fingers flipping the pages of his *Selected Poems*.

Before that night, the portrait of Walcott imprinted on my mind was from the cover of a collection of critical essays. The photo dates from the late 1960s. In a dashiki and Afro, Walcott is the pensive, unflinching young poet of "A Far Cry From Africa" and "Codicil"—"How can I turn from Africa and live?" and "To change your language, you must change your life." The Walcott of Victoria was a stout octogenarian in a woolen cardigan, the poetry establishment's version of the elder statesman. He moved slowly, but there was an awareness in his heavy-browed eyes each time he peeked over his spectacles at the noisy gathering. He seemed at ease in the curiosity shop, unembarrassed, as if even this was strangely familiar. Embarrassment in this case would have been ungracious, and Walcott's wisdom manifested in a quiet acceptance of his hosts' good intentions.

I was eager to hear Walcott read, not least because for years now my response to his work has differed from my students'. Many of my students are smitten with Walcott at first blush. Even if they're puzzled by his poetry, they identify with its preoccupations: the search for a stable place in a fragmented world, for instance, and the need to draw upon many languages and traditions in the creation of a contemporary aesthetic. When they choose to write about him, they usually have to rein in their affections and check their tendency to see his struggles as unmediated reflections upon their own.

In contrast, I was no fan of Walcott after my first experiences of his work; my reasons never seemed adequate given all that he has accomplished, but they stuck nonetheless. I disliked his tendency to over-indulge in wordplay, allusion, and pronominal ambiguity, to overload a metaphor such that a stanza becomes a room bulging with bric-a-brac—worthy of the Empress in fact. The final stanza of an early poem, "The Flock," is an example. In a northern clime, the speaker has seen a flock of ducks flying south towards the temperate regions with which he identifies. His mind, the tropics, the Arctic, and the flock all undergo alchemical transmutations that recall, stylistically, poets such as Henry Vaughan and Thomas Traherne. In the end, "The Flock" turns out to be a poem about vocation, particularly Walcott's personal struggle to define himself as an African-Caribbean writer who embraces an English literary tradition:

> Till its annihilation may the mind
> reflect his fixity through winter, tropic,
> until that equinox when the clear eye
> clouds, like a mirror, without contradiction,
> greet the black wings that cross it as a blessing
> like the high, whirring flock that flew across
> the cold sky of this page when I began
> this journey by the wintry flare of dawn,
> flying by instinct to their secret places,
> both for their need and for my sense of season.

Every major image in the poem, and at least one new one, gets twisted back into the tight weave of this final stanza. Walcott is less an alchemist, as I just suggested, than a blacksmith: the material of the weave is metal, and here I would say his work is overwrought, a Gothic rood screen.

Writing about Walcott, one ends up following his lead and searching for metaphor, although he is fundamentally a narrative poet. Plot, character, and dialogue are a refining fire for his lyricism, such that his best lyrical moments manifest in his verse stories. Perhaps that explains his choice of "The Schooner *Flight*" at the Victoria reading. The narrator, Shabine, who is a proxy for the poet, tells a sailor's tale: a disillusioned misfit and rugged individualist goes to sea to find himself, and in the midst of a terrible storm, he recognizes the spiritual strength his home has instilled in him. The story itself is generic: upon leaving home, one discovers its significance and longs to return. But the voice of Walcott's narrator is a sonorous, poetical patois in loose blank verse lines that revitalize the familiar tale. Damning the storm, Shabine declares, "If we's to drong, we go drong," the patois bringing out the consonance latent in "we're going to drown." Shabine's ear—Walcott's ear—is matched by his eye. Describing the casuarinas, he writes, "You see them on the low hills of

Barbados/ bracing like windbreaks, needled for hurricanes,/ tracking, like mists, the cirrus of torn sails." Metaphor and allusion, as in "The Flock," are still essential, but Walcott has complete command of them, aided by the constraints of character. Like his creator, Shabine is a poet of Dutch, English, and African ancestry, concerned about his vocation and its purpose in the struggles of the Caribbean. But Shabine is no more (or less) Walcott than Prufrock is Eliot or Satan is Milton, which is to say that there is enough difference that the persona insures against nostalgia for an idealized lost history and liberates the poet to think outside the confines of the self as lyric subject. It was Walcott's most theatrical reading in Victoria. The bass brogue was his, but the expressive flare was Shabine's.

The contemporary poetry reading is, in the main, a decidedly non-theatrical event. Most of Walcott's performance was understated—a quiet, careful reading in which the text is meant to speak for itself, just in the poet's voice. That part is crucial: it's why we attend those typically sedate stagings, why we place a higher value on Walcott reading Walcott than, for instance, Laurence Fishburne or Anthony Hopkins reading Walcott. And it helps explain why the Victoria audience's warmest response followed the poet's reading of "Sea Canes," a simple, elegiac lyric of personal experience. In it, the poet has traveled half his life's journey, far enough along that, as he bluntly puts it in the opening line, "Half my friends are dead." Such directness is unusual in Walcott but characteristic of this elegy. Although he cannot resist one esoteric image, "the seraph lances of my faith," the metaphor of the sea canes develops organically, much like the daffodils of the Wordsworth lyric that seems to provide an unconscious model. What Walcott would have flash upon his inward eye, however, is not an idealized image. Rather, he claims that the sound and motion of the blowing sea canes brings back his lost friends "with faults and all, not nobler, just there." It's an admirable sentiment destined to elicit sighs and nods and approving applause. I don't mean to imply that Walcott read it for that reason, or that our response wasn't genuine. On the contrary: we hoped to hear the poet speak, and he spoke, seemingly to us.

That was how the rain-soaked young man summed it up in the Q&A session that followed "Sea Canes": "I feel that you spoke directly to me." The audience of the lyric enters into a shared experience with the poet. Lyric is not narrative, but we listeners tend to render it so by filling out lyric space with our stories. In the co-op with Walcott, affection could not only be felt but also expressed. Walcott is not a sentimental poet, which does not preclude his readers from developing powerful attachments, especially in the presence of the man himself. I am aware of how Romantic my language is here, how reactionary it must seem when my tribe of literary and cultural critics has rendered such concepts as "presence" and "author" suspect, even silly. But outside the lively debates of literature conferences or avant-garde poetry klatches, the humanity of the poet and the language of his work are not easily disentangled. A reader wants to draw close to her favorite authors, to hear and see them, to get their signatures. "Sentimental" was not always pejorative, and the word's etymological complexity, implicating not just the emotions but also the intellect and physical sensation, should remind us that to be touched by the poet and to be stimulated intellectually by her work derive from related desires. We have many means now to hear a writer's voice—Internet archives such as PennSound, Ubuweb, and the Poetry Foundation, as well as vaults of audio disc and tape recordings. From blogs and tweets, we have ready access to a poet's quotidian thoughts and ruminations on culture and politics. Her lectures and forums come to our desktops or cellphones through live feeds. The metaphor is suggestive, for our appetite is great and the table bountiful.

Hunger, touch, the sensation of hearing a unique voice—the truth is that at the Walcott reading, my polite applause belied my excitement about being near a poet whose work I'd studied for years, no matter my vexed relationship to him. The affective power of literature can break down the critic's guard. That is sometimes wanted, as I'm suggesting. However, when we draw too close to the poem and poet, or when we think that we have done so, we see neither of them whole. Nostalgia lurked near the door of the co-op that evening, and occasionally inserted a cloven hoof. Fantasies of common origins and universal languages, of the poet as a man speaking to men [sic], whitewash difference. Our certainty that Walcott spoke of us, as well as to us, threatened to make him inaudible.

This is where the independence of the text becomes critical. Neither poet nor reader can control it, and it will resist being reduced to our satisfaction. It will trouble the waters. In "The Schooner *Flight*," Shabine's language is tainted by colonialism. Bitter about his own marginalization, he has internalized white prejudice toward blacks. His attitude toward women is troglodytic. He is rather too fond of saying "nigger" and "bitch." When he spat out those words that night in Victoria, people squirmed, snickered uncomfortably, or sat stony-faced, suppressing reaction. Walcott's reading of "The Schooner *Flight*" was a performance in various voices—his own, Shabine's, other characters', and the poem's. That last voice, the poem's, eludes both character and poet. It exceeds the poet's expectations and creates the discomfiture and confusion that precede criticism. I asked nothing about "The Schooner *Flight*" during the Q&A, although questions were winding into a knot in my chest. I imagine that others felt this way but, like me, deferred discussion to the walk home, or tomorrow's class, or an essay.

Of islands, Muriel Rukeyser famously swears, "For God's sake they're connected underneath." Dive down far enough, and you'll find the wreckage of imperialism in Victoria's history as in Castries'. On either shore, Walcott's poetry matters because its sea grapes and whelks seem native. Walcott has objected to being classified a Caribbean poet, not because he disowns his region but because he doesn't believe his work to be limited by it. This is a common complaint among writers, usually in response to critics who, for good reason, argue that paying attention to ethnicity and gender has diversified what counts as literature. Once our eyes and ears have been opened, however, identity categories fade behind the art: its inventiveness and humanity. I do not mean to suggest that literature transcends history and politics. Rather, at its best, it transforms them by causing us to think creatively about such abstractions as "Caribbean" and "colonial," or any in the array of categories that critics and publishers and bookstores now use to organize literature. A student of mine once declared that he only read work by women of color. There are conditions in which such a limitation would be constructive. Robert Penn Warren and Cleanth Brooks could have benefited from a year's commitment to such a regime, as would anyone convinced either that color and gender do not matter in writing, or that "women of color" speak with a unified voice. Sooner or later, the best poetry will break free of our restrictions upon it and recombine unpredictably. "Sea Canes" will transplant and thrive along the Pacific rim of Canada.

A few months after the Victoria conference and Walcott reading, my family and I were making our way down the Trans-Canada Highway on the opposite coast, in Nova Scotia. Our destination was Lockeport and a week with my wife's parents and sister, but we happened to drive by Great Village during the weekend of the Elizabeth Bishop Centenary celebration, the culmination of a year's worth of readings, concerts, memorials, and writing contests. I have described the setting of the Walcott event as "sincere." Imagine the earnestness of Bishop admirers who had made a pilgrimage to this remote crossroads in rural Nova Scotia. It was matched only by the determination of the hosts to claim Bishop, arguably the most itinerant 20th-century poet, as a Canadian maritimer. Bishop lived roughly three years in Great Village with her maternal grandparents, and her poetry and letters evidence just how formative those years were. But she is no more Nova Scotian than she is Floridian, Bostonian, or Brazilian. Her work is international in a way best described by critic Homi Bhabha, who claims that the assimilated prefix "inter," signifying "between," "carries the burden of the memory of culture." Bishop does not belong everywhere, but neither does she belong to a single geographical or national space.

The maritimers' bid for Bishop was familiarly Canadian. Surely no modern nation state is more ambivalent about national identity: on the one hand proud of itself as a "mosaic" of immigrant cultures rather than a "melting pot," on the other anxious that "What is Canadian?" is contingent, debatable and interesting only to (some) Canadians. Canadians scoff at American exceptionalism, but their most common conversation starter is, "Did you know that she/he/it (Margaret Atwood/Lorne Greene/the Space Shuttle Arm or the victor of the War of 1812) is Canadian?" If Canadians despair of being always in the shadows of the U.S. empire, maritimers bristle when they're compared to the supposedly cosmopolitan provinces of Quebec and Ontario. Nova Scotia, "Canada's Ocean Playground," has traditionally been cast as its provincial hinterland, less exotic than the far flung Newfies, but too far from Toronto to generate high culture. It's a land of coal, blueberries, and cod cheeks (at least before the sea was fished out). It's produced a few hockey players (but what province hasn't?), fiddlers, Anne Murray, and a prime minister of some renown. Now, at the centenary of Bishop's birth, Nova Scotia reproduced "our Elizabeth," headlining websites and brochures with a quip from one of her letters: "I am 3/4th Canadian, and 1/4th New Englander—I had ancestors on both sides of the Revolutionary War." At the Centenary Festival, "Canadian" stood for Nova Scotian, the whole for its essential part.

Although taking Bishop for Nova Scotia was a familiar, essentially benign act of small-scale Canadian imperialism, the festival's leaders could, in at least one respect, truly claim kinship with the poet. Their knowledge of her life and work was intricate and impassioned, similar to the way one knows a beloved relative or the landscape of home. For several months before our trip, I had read the Centenary blog. There were detailed accounts of the lives of Bishop's Great Village relatives, poetic responses to her poetry, fresh interpretations of musical settings of her work, deeply personal professions of debt to her voice, which had seemed to speak for a range of people. Bishop was like the map she famously describes in her early poem by that name, the inviting representation of a place we want to know, to study, to be acquainted with intimately. Bishop's map combines absolute precision and scope for imaginative flight. "Are they assigned," she asks, "or can the countries pick their colors?" Our urge to know Bishop so thoroughly would disturb her, for she shied away from public inquiry into her private affairs. She was given to self-doubt and skeptical of the self-exploration that was characteristic of the poetry of her contemporaries. Her reserve and humility, which we hear in recordings of her readings and witness even in her most critical correspondence with Robert Lowell, have helped make her a popular artist in a way that she is unlikely to have anticipated. She has moved into that unenviable class of poets whom people want to take care of: the forlorn Keats, reclusive Dickinson, mad John Clare . . . . geniuses all, whose reputations blossomed posthumously, and whose poetry gets entangled in our curiosity about their illness and secrecy and disappointment.

Across the road from the home of Bishop's Grandmother Bulmer is St. James United Church, an elegant, steepled, white clapboard building, iconic image of the North Atlantic village center. During Bishop's preschool years in Great Village, a Presbyterian congregation worshiped there. It wasn't Bishop's church. Recall that when she confronts a seal in "At the Fishhouses," Bishop realizes that they are both "believers in total immersion." Grace Bulmer was Baptist, and Bishop loved the hymns, though it is a Lutheran chestnut she names in the poem, and it's a Presbyterian minister and church steeple that we find in her "In the Village." Bishop was to give up her faith, but she never silenced her guilty conscience: a stern Protestant, frowning on her lack of self-discipline and her tendency to anesthetize her sorrows and disappointments with alcohol. In her modernization of a Christian parable, "The Prodigal," Bishop identifies with the self-exiled prodigal son, an alcoholic who resists the shame and humility of penitence, even as he begins to "come to himself." That is the King James Version's language, which Bishop refashions as "shuddering insights, beyond his control" brought on by the flight of bats over his head in the evening. In Jesus' parable, the prodigal returns to his father's house. But Bishop alters this. "You can't go home again" is a commonplace that Bishop's life and work painfully tested. Displacement, the permanence of it, looms against the horizon like the church steeple over the returning unbeliever. Bishop leaves her prodigal in a state of perpetual doubt, despite his decision to return to his father. "But it took him a long time," she concludes, "finally to make his mind up to go home." His mind is made up, but does he go? Home may not be there—will not, in fact, in the form that he recalls. Returning requires compromise and a will to settle, even after kneeling for forgiveness. To rephrase another Bishop line, might it be better to stay here and think of home?

On the exterior of St. James is a plaque in memory of Bishop, with the line "Home-made, home-made! But aren't we all?" from her late dramatic monologue "Crusoe in England." The homily at St. James on the Sunday of the Bishop Centenary was a quiet, thoughtful meditation on the universal need of a home. Raised Southern Baptist, I am prone to distraction in all but the most distressingly censorious sermons, so my mind kept wandering away to Crusoe's island. Bishop's version is a "cloud dump," redolent of "goat and guano." It has "one kind of everything," but this merely contributes to its monotony. Nonetheless the island becomes Crusoe's home, a land where he manages to carve a "home-made flute" and (unlike Defoe's otherwise master craftsman) make "home-brew." It's in a drunken revelry that Crusoe croons the lines inscribed on St. James. "Awful, fizzy, stinging stuff," home brew is generally made palatable by the pride of the brewer rather than the quality of the beverage. The imperfections of a homemade product are always offset by the charm of its being homemade. The central irony of Bishop's poem is that the castaway discovers upon returning to England that the unnamed Caribbean island made him. It was his true home, and it now has the insubstantial quality of a map image and fading memory. The objects most closely identified with his island—flute, knife, parasol—have become museum pieces, emptied of significance, or rather, their significance has been rendered historical and merely factual. At the same time, Crusoe's birth home, the English island from which he originated, is just "another island." Whatever its historical and global significance, England matters to the aging Crusoe only in relation to the other islands he has claimed a portion of. They are connected underneath, literally, but the meaningful connections are made closer to the surface by the art of memory. Bishop's revision of the Crusoe myth proposes that home and homeland are imaginary places, partial fabrications of the expatriate, the exile, the prodigal, and simply anyone who moved away. Great Village is significant to Bishop because she left it early and returned only sporadically. The most fulfilling visits were carried out in verse.

Salman Rushdie argues that the expatriate writer creates "imaginary homelands," reconstructions from shards of memory and fictions, intended and unintended. The fictiveness and fragmentation are what make the imaginary homeland instructive, not only to the writer but also to the reader who has remained in the land of her birth. Bishop's readers never, in my experience, dwell on the inaccuracies of her Great Village or Key West or Ouro Preto. We don't ask a poet to be accurate, just truthful, and I suspect that the organizers and patrons of the Elizabeth Bishop Centenary Festival stood in awe of the truth and beauty of her Nova Scotias of the mind. Her Nova Scotia was theirs, just as she was theirs and Walcott had belonged to the Canadian west-coast islanders.

In a classroom, where most people's experience of poetry begins and ends, we generally leave affection at the door. When orienting ourselves to a poet's work, our coordinates are period and nation, gender and ethnicity, school or group, predominant style or poetics. That is to say, we draw on the discipline to situate the poet and her work in a known landscape at some distance from ourselves. We sketch a map for reading, and as we explore the work, we recalculate and fill in the details. That's as it should be, arguably, since critical analysis of one kind or another is the primary mode and fundamental agenda of the institutional space, literature class. But in my experience, for all students, including the occasional would-be scholars, literature remains a dark, forbidding forest, a no-man's-land, until they encounter a writer who astonishes them and makes them want to follow. "I love that one," she says. "It's as if he knew me," he claims. She is ours. He speaks to me. Whether such affection can be sustained after the critical faculties have been exercised is doubtful, but it is what connects all readers of literature underneath.

BOOK REVIEW

Hollis Seamon

Eight Stories In Search of an Editor

A Review of Jacob M. Appel, *Scouting for the Reaper*

Black Lawrence Press, 2014

ISBN 978-1-1937854-95-9 (Paperback), USA $15.95

★ ★ ★

Jacob M. Appel writes an excellent story. This collection, winner of the Hudson Prize from Black Lawrence Press, contains eight fine fictions. Each story is substantial, twenty to thirty pages; each develops a full cast of characters; each delivers an engaging plot with a satisfying ending. Appel's dialogue is always spot-on and his stories portray the emotional complexities of truly human characters. His language is witty in the best sense: precise, clever and gently playful.

Appel is also a versatile writer, able to create, in this collection, both male and female narrators of all ages, all believable. The first three stories in the book use first-person narration by adolescents, two female and one male. The next three stories are told from the points of view of elderly female narrators, using close third-person narration. The last two stories are told in first person again, but this time by middle-aged men. This kind of deft literary ventriloquism makes sense, coming from a writer who is himself the very epitome of versatility. Appel is a physician, attorney, and bioethicist who holds advanced degrees in an astonishing number of disciplines, including BA and MA from Brown, MFA in fiction from NYU, MS in bioethics from Albany Medical College, PhD from Columbia, MD from Columbia, and JD from Harvard Law School. He's published more than two hundred short stories, and five books (two each in 2012 and 2014, with one in 2013). He publishes widely in the field of bioethics and his essays have appeared in many newspapers, including the *New York Times* and *Chicago Tribune*. He is, apparently, the kind of guy who makes Joyce Carol Oates look like a slacker.

So, given the skills and experience of this writer, is *Scouting for the Reaper* a truly wonderful collection of short stories? Alas, not quite. It *could* have been, if only Appel trusted his readers a bit more, not pushing points that intelligent readers would probably prefer to pick up on their own. And, even more crucial, the book could have been a far better collection, if only it had been edited and arranged more carefully. There is an art to creating a collection of stories, producing an effective fictional collage in which each piece illuminates and enriches the others and in which there is both coherence and variety. Here, it seems that no one took the time to make the collection as a whole as artful and entertaining as each story is, on its own.

But before we get to the flaws in the overall design, let's take a look at some of the individual stories and some elements that connect them. The title story has an all-time great first line: "Nothing sells tombstones like a Girl Scout in uniform." And the story delivers on this initial promise, presenting a young girl who is asked by her part-entrepreneur, part-con-man father, Gordon, to don a Girl Scout uniform (even though she's never belonged to that organization) and pretend to be an eleven-year-old scout (even though she's really thirteen and busting out of the traditional green vest). The girl, Natalie, allows herself to be even more deeply disguised by allowing the mother of a boy she's interested in to call her "Natasha" and by hoping that the boy, who is blind, will somehow find her, the self-described "ugliest thirteen-year-old in the eighth grade," beautiful. And Gordon models duplicity for his daughter. He is underhanded, if not downright deceptive, in his treatment of both his ex-wife, to whom he hopes to sell a tombstone, and his current wife, who deeply resents his attentions to the ex, telling him, "This is the *last* time that you're going over there. *The last!* If you go over again, you'll come home to an empty house." Yet, all the while he is shamelessly using all of the female characters simply to make a sale, Natalie's father continues to declare that he is behaving in a perfectly honest way. He has the last word, in the final sentence: "Honestly, it's the most reasonable deal around."

This desire to *seem* perfectly trustworthy, even when engaging in some pretty dubious behavior, is characteristic of many of the characters in the collection, one of a number of chords that resonate and echo among the stories. In "Choose Your Own Genetics," a father who knows perfectly well that the girl he calls his daughter is probably the child of another man, defies science to convince her that the blood evidence is wrong: "'Blood type means nothing. *Nothing*'." A trucker who is harboring a teenage stowaway in his rig, a girl he fears will say something to get him "hauled off to Leavenworth," tries to convince a diner waitress that everything is on the up-and-up in "Hazardous Cargoes" by pretending to be the girl's father. In "Ad Valorem," an accountant who's done some dicey number-crunching convinces the widow of his client that he's done nothing wrong: "Felix Ingersoll smiled down on her nervously. His big dark eyes were tender, desperate, longing—anything but those of a thief."

Blindness also recurs throughout the collection, both in the physical and metaphorical sense. It is Lucien's lack of sight, in "Scouting for the Reaper," that allows Natalie to become far more daring than she's ever been, shedding her clothes to swim with him and, for the first time, dropping her false identity: "Then I dove into the water, wearing only my underwear, looking as unlike a Girl Scout as anyone has ever been." And, yet, Lucien's blindness also forces her to confront her true self-doubt: "Or maybe Lucien's greatest sin was being blind—liking me for who I was, rather than finding me alluring." In the end, Natalie uses Lucien's lack of sight to leave him, abruptly disappearing without explanation: "'Where are you going?' demanded Lucien. I didn't answer. I slipped into the hallway, indifferent, letting him pepper the empty room with his questions." "Rods and Cones" begins with blindness: "Another family crisis. The rabbit goes blind." The main character, Roberta, has an ailment much like the rabbit's, suffering spells that she calls "lapses" and her doctor calls pseudo-seizures. Her lapses are not detectable by EEG; they are part of a somatoform disorder that only *feels* real, her doctor tells her. The rabbit's blindness (also, probably psychosomatic) reveals to Roberta the source of her own marital discontent: ". . . . it isn't just the rabbit's eyesight. It's her husband's attitude toward the rabbit's eyesight. *His resignation to the blindness.* She is married to a man who chuckles off tragedy, be it hers or the rabbit's. . . ." Greta, the lonely and love-struck widow in "Ad Valorem," chooses to remain blind to the dishonesty of the accountant who has both robbed and charmed her, allowing him to toss the evidence she's painstakingly collected into the sea. In these stories, characters' blindness reveals their deeper fears and pushes them toward the climactic moments of confrontation and/or resignation.

There are other threads woven nicely among these stories, connections that readers will enjoy discovering. But within the stories, Appel's tendency to over-explain his symbolism too often destroys the pleasure of discovery. He seems determined to negate the stereotype of the too-subtle MFA workshop story by being anything *but* subtle. In "Rods and Cones," for example, the reader is just beginning to understand how profoundly Roberta has replaced her grown children with her beloved rabbit, when Appel makes sure we can't miss this point, inserting an unnecessary explanatory phrase into the sentence, "She has only one rabbit—one family—and she's entitled to protect it." And in case we've somehow missed the ways in which Roberta anthropomorphizes her rabbit, Appel gives her an all-too-appropriate book to read in a waiting room: *Watership Down*. In "The Extinction of Fairy Tales," the elderly, frail Edie, a fairy tale researcher and scholar, spends time imagining the life of her mysterious missing gardener and then states, supposedly as a startling revelation, something the reader has most certainly already realized: "Making up Sammy's life was like writing a fairy tale." When, at the start of "Creve Coeur," a character says, "Whatever. As long as you don't electrocute yourself," you can bet that someone will electrocute himself—and, yes, he does. These instances when Appel seems to doubt his readers' intelligence and perspicuity are small but irritating disappointments.

A much larger flaw in the collection is that of redundancies and repetitions among stories, the kinds of things that should have been caught, if not by the author himself, then certainly by an astute editor. Of course, all writers have images they return to, little tics of language, character, and plot that are not apparent when reading a single story. But when these tics pop up in a number of stories, it seems like editorial carelessness. For example, in three separate stories, a man uses the exact same gesture to comfort his wife. "Dad parted her bangs and kissed her on the forehead" ("Creve Coeur," p. 38). "Then my father brushed aside Mama's gray-tinged bangs, kissed her on the forehead" ("Scouting for the Reaper," p. 55). "He kissed Roberta on the forehead, between her silver-streaked bangs" ("Rods and Cones," p. 109). The reader experiences disorienting déjà vu as this gesture reappears, in different families, in different stories. Where am I, we ask? What story am I in? Is it Groundhog Day?

And this odd déjà-vu-all-over-again effect is established early in the collection, where the second and third stories have weirdly similar plots and characters. In both "Creve Coeur" and "Scouting for the Reaper," adolescent narrators follow their fathers into the homes of former lovers (one an ex-wife, one an ex-fiancée); both narrators fall in love with the ex's child; both of the exes are dying. The only real difference is the gender of the narrator: male in "Creve Coeur," female in "Scouting for the Reaper."

Reading these two stories, placed next to each other in the collection, is disconcerting.

There are other instances of inadvertent repetition and awkward juxtaposition. The first three stories present families of adolescents whose parents are experiencing marital difficulty and keeping secrets. The next trio of stories all center on older women who have lost large parts of themselves, along with loved ones. The final pair of stories shows middle-aged men trying to negotiate complex human relationships while also dealing with practical problems that are comically absurd. The narrator of "Hazardous Cargoes" is transporting a truckload of penguins while the narrator of "The Vermin Episode" struggles with how to bury Gregor Samsa when no one will receive that creepy corpse. This grouping of stories into clumps of similarity is hardly the most effective or creative arrangement.

Perhaps we're not meant to read the stories in the order in which they appear? Perhaps the order is awry to start with? (After all, the table of contents lists two stories as "3," creating an initial jarring note of confusion.) Perhaps we're meant not to notice the odd repetitions of images, plot lines and even character names (two different Natalies in the first three stories)? Perhaps we're meant to forget one story the minute we begin the next? Perhaps we're not meant to be careful readers?

Perhaps. But that would be a shame. Jacob Appel's stories deserve careful readers. Each tale is cleverly constructed and well-told. Jacob Appel is an excellent writer whose stories deserve a more persnickety editor.

AbleMUSE
A REVIEW OF POETRY, PROSE & ART

After more than a decade of online publishing excellence, Able Muse began a bold new chapter with its print edition

We continue to bring you in print the usual masterful craft with poetry, fiction, essays, art & photography, and book reviews

Check out our 12+ years of online archives for work by

RACHEL HADAS • X.J. KENNEDY • TIMOTHY STEELE • MARK JARMAN • A.E. STALLINGS • DICK DAVIS • A.M. JUSTER • TIMOTHY MURPHY • DEBORAH WARREN • CHELSEA RATHBURN • RHINA P. ESPAILLAT • TURNER CASSITY • RICHARD MOORE • STEPHEN EDGAR • ANNIE FINCH • THAISA FRANK • NINA SCHUYLER • SOLITAIRE MILES • MISHA GORDIN • & SEVERAL OTHERS

SUBSCRIPTION
Able Muse – Print Edition - Subscriptions:

Able Muse is published semiannually.

Subscription rates, for individuals: $24.00 per year; single and previous issues: $16.95 + $3 S&H.

International subscription rates: $33 per year; single and previous issues: $16.95 + $5 S&H.
(All rates in USD.)

Subscribe online with WePay/credit card **www.ablemusepress.com**

Or send a check payable to *Able Muse Review*
Attn: Alex Pepple - Editor, Able Muse, 467 Saratoga Avenue #602, San Jose, CA 95129 USA

New From

Cup
poems by **Jeredith Merrin**
SPECIAL HONOREE - 2013 ABLE MUSE BOOK AWARD

978-1-927409-34-3 | Paperback

". . . stanzas, rooms, lives./ And you, toiling to make it better,/ whatever your it is./ Each has a cup."

In these forthright and moving poems written in restrained, disciplined stanzas, the stories are told of how we each, "trying to make it better,/ whatever . . . it is," have to find our own cup, and find it acceptable.
—David Ferry

In Cup we meet a poet of rare power and unique originality, unafraid of feeling, able to take on matters of the deepest consequence.
—X.J. Kennedy, Judge for the 2013 Able Muse Book Award

All the Wasted Beauty of the World
poems by **Richard Newman**
FINALIST - 2012 ABLE MUSE BOOK AWARD

978-1-927409-31-2 | Paperback

All the Wasted Beauty of the World is masterful and magnetic . . . Newman's poems, with their formal, lapidary precision, their indelible portraits of life in the cheap bars, back alleys, and rough hewn edges of the Midwest, surprise a hunger in us for a language larger, wilder, and unabashedly loftier than daily speech.
—George Bilgere

All the Wasted Beauty of the World returns us to the real and, consequently, the new by putting on the brakes and asking us to look, if only briefly, beyond our rear-views.
—Dorianne Laux

Details at

ABLE MUSE PRESS

Vellum
poems by **Chelsea Woodard**
FINALIST - 2013 ABLE MUSE BOOK AWARD

978-1-927409-35-0 | Paperback

The honed music here thus reveals a deeper vulnerability.
—Bruce Bond

Not the least of the attractions of this gifted young poet's first book is the exquisite, searing precision of her language . . . I predict for Chelsea Woodard a long and enviable career.
—B.H. Fairchild

In addition to her emotional maturity, part of what makes these poems memorable is Woodard's obvious mastery of language, her flawless sentences.
—Claudia Emerson, from the foreword

Greed: A Confession
poems by **D.R. Goodman**
FINALIST - 2013 ABLE MUSE BOOK AWARD

978-1-927409-38-1 | Paperback

All the Wasted Beauty of the World is This poet is alive to everything. You want this book. It's terrific.
—Kelly Cherry

Goodman is greedy for things of this world—not in the rapacious, bottom-line manner . . . but for the enlightenment of the senses and the enrichment of her poetry. She's sharing the wealth she accumulates.
—John Drury, from the foreword

Complex yet accessible, these formal and free-verse poems gift us with abundant insights to enjoy.
—Beth Houston

www.AbleMusePress.com

TRANSLATION NOTES

Cartel pour le combat à cheval, en forme de balet

Ces nouveaux Chevaliers par moy vous font entendre
Que leurs premiers ayeuls furent fils de Méandre,
À qui le fleuve apprit à tourner leurs chevaux
Comme il tourne et se vire et se plie en ses eaux.

Pyrrhe en celle façon sur le tombeau d'Achille
Feit une danse armée, et aux bords de Sicile
Enée en decorant son pere de tournois,
Feit sauter les Troyens au branle du harnois,
Où les jeunes enfans en cent mille manieres
Meslerent les replis de leurs courses guerrières.

Pallas qui les conduit, a de sa propre main
Façonné leurs chevaux, et leur donna le frein,
Mais plustost un esprit, qui sagement les guide
Par art, obeissant à la loy de la bride.

Tantost vous les voirrez à courbettes danser,
Tantost se reculer, s'approcher, s'avancer,
S'escarter, s'esloigner, se serrer, se rejoindre
D'une pointe allongée, et tantost d'une moindre,
Contrefaisant la guerre au semblant d'une paix,
Croisez, entrelassez de droit et de biais,
Tantost en forme ronde, et tantost en carrée,
Ainsi qu'un Labyrinth, dont la trace esgarée
Nous abuse les pas en ses divers chemins,

Ainsi qu'on voit danser en la mer les Dauphins,
Ainsi qu'on voit volet par le travers des nues
En diverses façons une troupe de Grues.

— *Pierre de Ronsard*
(Original French version, abridged)

Femme et chatte

Elle jouait avec sa chatte;
Et c'était merveille de voir
La main blanche et la blanche patte
S'ébattre dans l'ombre du soir.

Elle cachait—la scélérate!—
Sous ces mitaines de fil noir
Ses meurtriers ongles d'agate,
Coupants et clairs comme un rasoir.

L'autre aussi faisait la sucrée,
Et rentrait sa griffe acérée,
Mais le diable n'y perdait rien...

Et dans le boudoir où, sonore,
Tintait son rire aérien,
Brillaient quatre points de phosphore.

— *Paul Verlaine*
 (Original French version)

Award Winners from

Corporeality
~ Stories by Hollis Seamon ~
978-1-927409-03-9 | Paperback

- **Gold Medal winner, 2014 Independent Book Publisher Outstanding Book Award**
- **Finalist, 2013 Foreword Review's Best Book of the Year**

"Seamon offers enough thematic and narrative variation to keep each story in this collection fresh." — *Publishers Weekly*

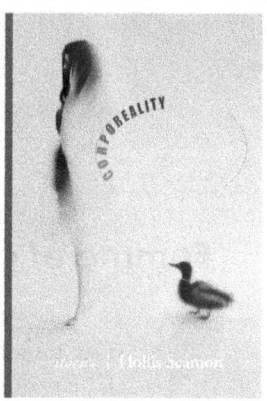

Sailing to Babylon
~ poems by **James Pollock** ~
978-0-9865338-7-7 | Paperback

- **Winner, Outstanding Achievement Award in Poetry from the Wisconsin Library Association**
- **Finalist, 2013 Griffin Poetry Prize**
- **Finalist, 2012 Governor General's Literary Award in Poetry**
- **Honorable Mention, 2012 Posner Poetry Book Award**

"A rich and complex array of subjects and allusions to provide both pleasure and challenge" — *Pleiades: A Journal of New Writing*

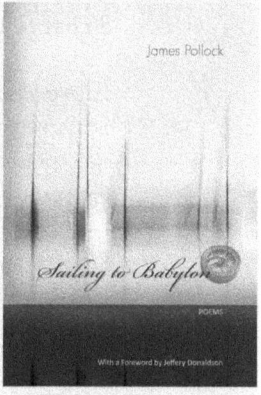

Strange Borderlands
~ Poems by Ben Berman ~
978-1-927409-05-3 | Paperback

- **Winner, 2014 Peace Corps Writers Best Book Award**
- **Finalist, 2014 Massachusetts Book Award**

"This is a must-have book for readers of poetry."
— *Publishers Weekly*, starred review

Life in the Second Circle
~ Poems by Michael Cantor ~
978-0-9878705-5-1 | Paperback

- **Finalist, 2013 Massachusetts Book Award**

"A sensory kaleidoscope where the poems are more like movies."
— Deborah Warren

Able Muse Press // www.ablemusepress.com

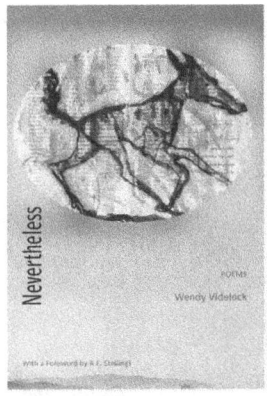

Nevertheless
~ Poems by Wendy Videlock ~

978-0-9865338-4-6 | Paperback

- **Finalist, 2012 Colorado Book Award**

"Videlock is a magician of play and pleasures, wisdom being not the least of these." — A.E. Stallings

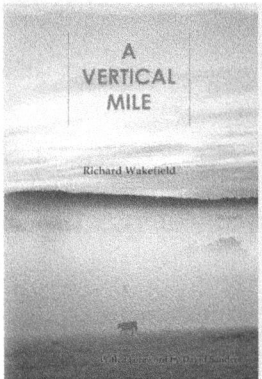

A Vertical Mile
~ Poems by Richard Wakefield ~

978-0-9878705-7-5 | Paperback

- **Shortlisted, 2014 Poets Prize**

"Wakefield crafts his verse to exacting standards yet keeps it uncontrived." — David Sanders

The Cosmic Purr
~ Poems by Aaron Poochigian ~

978-0-9878705-2-0 | Paperback

- **Shortlisted, 2014 Poets Prize**

"Aaron Poochigian's technique is masterly . . . and it's easy to be beguiled by these poems' wit and bravura. But the pyrotechnics are used to serious ends." — Dick Davis

Lines of Flight
~ Poems by Catherine Chandler ~

978-0-9865338-3-9 | Paperback

- **Shortlisted, 2013 Poets Prize**

"Lines of Flight is altogether a lively performance." — Richard Wilbur

Able Muse Book Award Winners

Walking in on People
~ poems by **Melissa Balmain** ~

Winner - 2013 Able Muse Book Award
Selected by X.J. Kennedy
978-1-927409-29-9 | Paperback

Melissa Balmain's poems add to the rhythmic bounce of light verse a darker, more cutting humor. The result is an infectious, often hilarious blend of the sweet and the lethal, the charming and the acidic.
— Billy Collins

Virtue, Big as Sin
~ poems by **Frank Osen** ~

Winner - 2012 Able Muse Book Award
Selected by Mary Jo Salter
978-1-927409-16-9 | Paperback

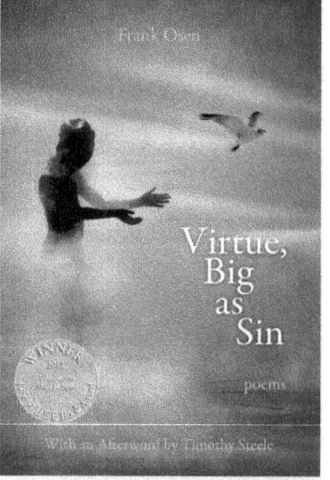

In his talent for tragedy and comedy, and for mixing them, Osen takes his place in a distinguished line of English-language poets that runs from Chaucer and Shakespeare down to our day.
—Timothy Steele (from the afterword)

Dirge for an Imaginary World
~ poems by **Matthew Buckley Smith** ~

Winner - 2011 Able Muse Book Award
Selected by Andrew Hudgins
978-0-9878705-0-6 | Paperback

The range of subjects is equally and as charmingly eclectic, from Neanderthals, Dante, Vermeer, for instance, to College Football Mascots, Highway Mediums, and Spring Ballet Exams. Mental and linguistic agility generously challenge the reader in poem after poem.
— Greg Williamson (from the "Foreword")

Details at www.AbleMusePress.com

CONTRIBUTOR NOTES

A native of Wisconsin, BRIDGET APFELD is currently a student in the University of North Carolina-Wilmington's MFA program, where she specializes in fiction. Her work has appeared or is forthcoming in various literary journals, including *Dislocate, Prick of the Spindle, So to Speak, Better: Culture & Lit* and *Verse Wisconsin.*

PETER AUSTIN lives with his wife and three daughters in Toronto, Canada, where he teaches English at Seneca College. He has published three collections of poems and a short verse novel. A fourth collection, *The Acid Test,* will appear later in 2014. In a previous life, he wrote a musical version of *The Wind in the Willows,* which received four professional productions.

ROY BENTLEY has received fellowships from the NEA, the Florida Division of Cultural Affairs, and the Ohio Arts Council. Poems have appeared in *The Southern Review, Shenandoah, Pleiades, Blackbird, North American Review, Prairie Schooner* and elsewhere. Books include *Boy in a Boat* (University of Alabama, 1986), *Any One Man* (Bottom Dog, 1992), *The Trouble with a Short Horse in Montana* (White Pine, 2006), and *Starlight Taxi* (Lynx House 2013).

ERIC BERLIN grew up in suburban New Jersey during the 1980s with a love for storytelling instilled by his grandmother. He was drawn to poetry partly as a way of coping with her death. After studying English at Harvard, he joined an improv troupe to cultivate spontaneity within various comedic forms. Shifting from that collaborative creativity to a more individual sort, he earned a Sculpture MFA at NY Academy of Art and a Poetry MFA at Syracuse University, where he lives with his partner Ellen, her wonderful son Joah, and their newest family member Ezra. Eric edits freelance and is writing two books of his own: a book of poems and a study of poetic patterning in stand-up comedy.

CATHARINE SAVAGE BROSMAN, PhD, is Professor Emerita of French at Tulane University. She was Mellon Professor of Humanities for 1990 and later held the Gore Chair in French. She was also visiting professor for a term at the University of Sheffield, UK. Her scholarly publications comprise eighteen books on French literary history and criticism. A new volume, *Louisiana Creole Literature: A Historical Study,* has just been published. She has published two collections of personal essays and nine collections of verse, including *Under the Pergola* (2011) and *On the North Slope* (2012). Her tenth collection, *On the Old Plaza,* has just been released. New poems and essays are out or forthcoming in *The South Carolina Review, Sewanee Review, Measure, Modern Age,* and *Southwest Review.*

DUANE CAYLOR is a physician in Dubuque, Iowa. His poetry has appeared or is forthcoming in various journals, most recently *Blue Unicorn, American Arts Quarterly, Off the Coast, Atlanta Review,* and *First Things.* He has been a finalist for both the Morton Marr Poetry Prize and the Nemerov Sonnet Award, and he received honorable mention for the Frost Farm Prize in 2014.

CATHERINE CHANDLER is an American poet, teacher and translator. She is the author of *Lines of Flight* (Able Muse Press, 2011), shortlisted for the 2013 Poets' Prize, *This Sweet Order* (White Violet Press/Kelsay Books, 2012) and *Glad and Sorry Seasons* (Bibliaosis, 2014), as well as two chapbooks, *For No Good Reason* and *All or Nothing.* Winner of the 2010 Howard Nemerov Sonnet Award, Catherine's poems, translations, essays, podcasts and interviews have been widely published in journals and anthologies in North America, Europe and Australia. She currently lives in Saint-Lazare, Quebec, and Punta del Este, Uruguay.

TERESE COE's poems and translations have appeared in *Poetry, The Threepenny Review, Ploughshares, New American Writing, Alaska Quarterly Review, The Cincinnati Review, Smartish Pace, Tar River Poetry* and *The Huffington Post;* in the UK, *The TLS, Poetry Review, Agenda, New Walk Magazine, Orbis,* and *Warwick Review;* in Ireland, *The Stinging Fly;* and in many other publications, including anthologies. She has written several plays, including *Harry Smith at the Chelsea Hotel,* about the celebrated collector of *The Anthology of American Folk Music,* filmmaker, and wit. Copies of her poem "More" were heli-dropped across London as part of the 2012 London Olympics' Poetry Parnassus.

Since his retirement from university teaching, MICHAEL COHEN has been writing personal essays. Almost two dozen of these, including "The Place Where It Happened," have just been collected in *A Place to Read: Life and Books,* published by Interactive Publications in Brisbane. He is the author of five other books, including an introductory poetry text, *The Poem in Question* (Harcourt Brace, 1983); an award-winning book on Shakespeare's *Hamlet* (Georgia, 1989); and a book about mystery fiction, *Murder Most Fair* (Associated University Presses, 2000). He lives in Murray, Kentucky, and Tucson, Arizona.

KATHARINE COLES's fifth poetry collection, *The Earth Is Not Flat* (Red Hen, 2013), was written under the auspices of the National Science Foundation's Antarctic Artists and Writers Program; ten poems from the book, translated into German by Klaus Martens, appeared in the summer 2014 issue of the journal *Matrix.* Her sixth collection, *Flight,* is due out in 2016. Recent poems and prose have appeared in *Poetry Northwest, Seneca Review, Virginia Quarterly Review, Image, Crazyhorse, Ascent,* and *Poetry*. A professor at the University of Utah, in 2009–2010 she served as the inaugural director of the Poetry Foundation's Harriet Monroe Poetry Institute. She has received grants and awards from the NEA, the NEH and the Guggenheim Foundation.

Robert W. Crawford lives in Chester, NH. He has published two books of poetry, *The Empty Chair,* winner of the 2011 Richard Wilbur Award, and *Too Much Explanation Can Ruin a Man*. His poems, "Odds Are" and "The Empty Chair," won the 2011 and 2006 Howard Nemerov Sonnet Award. His work has appeared in *Measure, The Formalist, First Things, Dark Horse, The Raintown Review, The Lyric, Forbes,* and many other journals. He is a trustee of the Robert Frost Farm in Derry, NH, a long-time member of the Powow River Poets, and cofounder of the Hyla Brook Poets. He teaches social studies, and is the JV Head Football coach at Pelham High School in Pelham, NH.

Born and bred in New Jersey, Frank De Canio works in New York. He loves music from Bach to Dory Previn, Amy Beach to Amy Winehouse, World Music, Latin, opera. He attends a philosophy workshop on 23rd Street, New York City, and is a fan of foreign film and a student of psychoanalysis. Shakespeare is his consolation, writing his hobby. He likes Dylan Thomas, Keats, Wallace Stevens, Frost, Ginsberg, and Sylvia Plath as poets. He presently holds an Associate's degree in liberal arts and has been published in diverse magazines in print and online. He's written more than 1500 poems, mostly sonnets.

Tamas Dobozy is a professor at Wilfrid Laurier University. He has published three books of short fiction, *When X Equals Marylou, Last Notes and Other Stories,* and *Siege 13: Stories,* the last of which won the 2012 Rogers' Writers Trust of Canada Fiction Prize and was shortlisted for the 2012 Governor General's Award for Fiction. He has published over 50 stories in North American and British journals including *Fiction, AGNI, One Story,* and *Granta,* and won an O. Henry Prize in 2011. He lives in Kitchener, Ontario, Canada.

Derek Furr is a literature professor and director of the Master of Arts in Teaching Program at Bard College. He is the author of a collection of fiction and essays, *Suite For Three Voices* (Fomite Press, 2012), and a work of literary criticism, *Recorded Poetry and Poetic Reception from Edna Millay to the Circle of Robert Lowell* (Palgrave Macmillan, 2010). *Semitones,* a new collection of prose and poetry with art by Andres San Millan, will be published by Fomite in 2015.

After her Tulsa upbringing and with a psychology degree from Vassar College, Diane Furtney worked a year in Israel (1967), then took an assortment of jobs, sometimes in clinical psychology, in several U.S. cities. Besides nonfiction ghostwriting, she has authored two prize-winning poetry chapbooks *(Destination Rooms* and *It Was a Game)* and two comic mystery novels (pseudonym D.J.H. Jones). Her poems and translations (French, Japanese) are in numerous journals in the U.S. and England, including

The Virginia Quarterly Review, The Iowa Review, Poetry International, Circumference and *Stand.* A full-length collection of science-based poems, *Science And,* was published in 2014 by FutureCycle Press. She now lives with her spouse, near Phoenix.

J.P. Grasser is originally from Maryland. His work explores the diverse regions he has called home, most insistently his family's fish hatchery in Brady, Nebraska. He studied English and Creative Writing at Sewanee: The University of the South and is currently an MFA student in poetry at Johns Hopkins University. His work appears or is forthcoming from *The Journal, Cream City Review, Ninth Letter Online, The Collagist,* and *Nashville Review,* among others.

R.S. Gwynn—See page 88.

Barbara Haas has an MFA from UC-Irvine, is an NEA Fellowship recipient (fiction) and teaches in the Creative Writing & Environment MFA program at Iowa State University. She is a repeat contributor to *The North American Review, Virginia Quarterly Review* and *The Hudson Review.* Her nonfiction centers on environmental issues in Russia.

Since winning *Southwest Review*'s Morton Marr Poetry Prize in 2008, Lisa Huffaker's poems have been published in *Southwest Review, Poet Lore, Measure, Southern Poetry Review, Mezzo Cammin, The Texas Observer,* and *Southern Humanities Review,* which recently nominated her for the Pushcart Prize. Lisa's primary background is classical singing; she holds a Master of Music degree in Vocal Performance from the New England Conservatory, and has sung with The Dallas Opera since 1999. She currently teaches creative writing at Yavneh Academy of Dallas.

Stephen Kampa has poems published or forthcoming in *Yale Review, Smartish Pace, Subtropics, Rattle, First Things, Cincinnati Review,* and others. His first book, *Cracks in the Invisible,* won the Hollis Summers Poetry Prize and a gold medal in poetry from the Florida Book Awards. His second book, *Bachelor Pad,* recently appeared from the Waywiser Press.

Len Krisak's latest books are *Afterimage, The Carmina of Catullus,* and *Ovid's Erotic Poems.* His work appears in the *Hudson, Sewanee, PN,* and *Antioch* reviews, and he is the recipient of the Robert Penn Warren, Richard Wilbur, and Robert Frost Prizes. He is also a four-time champion on *Jeopardy!*

Judith Kunst's poetry has appeared or is forthcoming in *The Atlantic, Poetry, Southern Poetry Review, Saint Katherine Review, In Posse, LUMINA, Measure,* and other publications. Her book, *The Burning Word* (Paraclete Press) explores the treasure houses of Jewish literary traditions and the Bible. She holds an MFA from Sarah Lawrence College and lives with her family at La Lumiere School in northwest Indiana.

MICHAEL LACARE grew up in Long Island, New York and moved to Florida when he was twenty-one. His essays and stories have appeared in numerous literary magazines. He lives in Florida with his wife and children, where he is currently at work on a novel.

DORIE DEWITT LARUE's first novel, *Resurrecting Virgil* (The Backwaters Press), won the Omaha Prize for Fiction. Her poetry collections include *The Private Frenzy* (University of Nebraska Press) and *Seeking the Monsters* (New Spirit Press). She is a recipient of a Louisiana DOA Fellowship, a Shreveport Regional Arts Council Fellowship, and four grants from the Louisiana Endowment for the Humanities. Her work has appeared in *The Southern Review, The American Poetry Review, The Massachusetts Review* and elsewhere. LaRue, a PhD in Creative Writing and Early American literature (University of Louisiana), has taught at Grambling State University and Louisiana State University in Baton Rouge, and presently teaches American literature at LSUS. She taught at IUBAT in Dhaka, Bangladesh (summer 2014).

HAILEY LEITHAUSER is the author of *Swoop* (Graywolf, 2013), which won the Poetry Foundation's 2012 Emily Dickinson First Book Award. She has recent or upcoming work in *Ecotone, Pleiades, Poetry, The Virginia Quarterly Review,* and *Best American Poetry 2014*. Last spring, she taught at The Writer's Center in Bethesda, MD.

KATHRYN LOCEY teaches English at Brenau University in Gainesville, Georgia. Most recently, her poems have appeared in *Paper Nautilus, Able Muse,* and the *Voices from the Porch* anthology.

DAVID MASON's latest collection is *Sea Salt: Poems of a Decade, 2004-2014*. His *Davey McGravy: Tales to Be Read Aloud to Children and Adult Children,* will be out early in 2015, illustrated by Grant Silverstein. A professor at Colorado College, he served as poet laureate of Colorado from 2010 to 2014, and divides his time between Colorado and Oregon.

ANTHONY MASTROIANNI lives in Rome.

MARTIN MCGOVERN earned his MA in philosophy at Stanford University and his PhD in creative writing/literature at the University of Houston's Creative Writing Program. His poetry, essays, and reviews have appeared in *The New Republic, Poetry, The Denver Quarter, Hotel Amerika, Chicago Review, Kenyon Review, Sewanee Review,* and elsewhere. Cofounder and codirector of the soon debuting Mile-High Low-Residency MFA at Regis University, where he currently teaches creative writing, literature and philosophy, McGovern's poetry collection, *Bad Fame,* will appear this winter with Able Muse Press.

SUSAN MCLEAN is an English professor at Southwest Minnesota State University. Her first poetry book, *The Best Disguise,* won the 2009 Richard Wilbur Award, and her second book, *The Whetstone*

Misses the Knife, won the 2014 Donald Justice Poetry Prize. *Selected Epigrams,* her translations of over five hundred Latin epigrams by Martial, will be published by the University of Wisconsin Press. Her poems and translations have appeared in *Measure, Mezzo Cammin, Arion, Transference, Light,* and elsewhere.

JEREDITH MERRIN, brought up in the Pacific Northwest, took her MA in English (specializing in Chaucer), and a PhD from UC Berkeley in Anglo-American Poetry and Poetics. *Cup,* a special honoree in the 2013 Able Muse Book Award, is her third collection; her previous books are *Shift* and *Bat Ode* (University of Chicago Press Phoenix Poets series). She's authored an influential book of criticism on Marianne Moore and Elizabeth Bishop. Her reviews and essays (on Moore, Bishop, Clare, Mew, Amichai, and others), and poems have appeared in *Paris Review, Slate, Ploughshares, Southwest Review, Yale Review* and elsewhere. A retired Professor of English (The Ohio State University), she lives near Phoenix.

TERESA MILBRODT is the author of the short story collection *Bearded Women: Stories* (Chizine Publications), the novel *The Patron Saint of Unattractive People (*Boxfire Press), and the flash fiction collection *Larissa Takes Flight: Stories* (Pressgang). Her stories, flash fiction and poems have appeared in numerous literary journals, and several have been nominated for a Pushcart Prize.

SCOTT M. MILLER earned a bachelor's degree in mathematics from M.I.T. and an MFA in poetry from Antioch University Los Angeles. His work has appeared in *Barrow Street, Raintown Review, Barefoot Muse* and other journals. When not working on poetry or developing software, Scott might be found in the kitchen kneading dough, outside practicing kung fu, or trying to teach himself Quantum Field Theory. He lives in Los Angeles with his wife and young son.

PIERRE DE RONSARD (1524 – 1585) was for many years the royal poet for the House of Valois, memorializing numerous kings and members of the French court as well as official events and literary figures, including Henri II, Charles IX, François Rabelais, and Marguerite de Navarre. Among the more than one thousand poems he wrote were sonnets on Petrarch, odes after Pindar and Horace, elegies, eclogues, songs, and witty if sometimes dark light verse. He investigates the metaphysical and the all-too-human, the obscure and the infinite, the subtle and the passionate, and organic and inorganic phenomena of the Earth. He openly advises the reader on how to comprehend and confront the world.

KYLE POTVIN's poetry has appeared in *The New York Times, Measure, The Huffington Post, JAMA, Blue Unicorn, Alimentum,* and on *BBC's World Update,* among others. She was named a finalist for the 2008 Howard Nemerov Sonnet Award. Her first collection of poetry, *Sound Travels on Water* (Finishing Line Press), co-won the 2014 Jean Pedrick Chapbook Award from the New England Poetry Club. She lives in Derry, NH, and helps coordinate the Robert Frost Farm's Hyla Brook Reading Series.

ZARA RAAB's latest book is *Fracas & Asylum* (David Robert Books). Earlier books are *Swimming the Eel*, and *The Book of Gretel* with narrative poems on the remote lost coast of northern California in an earlier, mythical time. Her work, including book reviews as well as poems, has appeared in *Verse Daily, River Styx, West Branch, Arts & Letters, Crab Orchard Review, Critical Flame, Prime Number, Raven Chronicles,* and *The Dark Horse*. She is a contributing editor to *Poetry Flash* and *The Redwood Coast Review*. *Rumpelstiltskin, or What's in a Name?* was a finalist for the Dana Award. She lives in Massachusetts.

JASON PHILLIP REESER, editor of Saint James Infirmary Books, lives and writes in southwest Louisiana. His ghost story anthology, *The Cities of the Dead,* which Louisiana Poet Laureate Julie Kane called "a twist of Louisiana Gothic," is set in the cemeteries of New Orleans. This year he published *Kiss of the Lazaretto,* the third book in his *Lazaretto* trilogy, which mixes science fiction and hard-boiled detective thrillers. His blog, *Room With No View,* has featured interviews with poets as well as fiction author David Morrell, the creator of Rambo. He lives in Louisiana with his wife, the poet Jennifer Reeser.

MAXINE ROSALER's fiction has appeared or is forthcoming in *The Southern Review, Glimmer Train, Fifth Wednesday,* and *New York Press*. She is a recipient of a New York Foundation for the Arts Fiction Fellowship and a story of hers was cited in an edition of *The Best American Short Stories*. She is also the author of a number of young adult nonfiction books. "The Uncle" is part of a collection of short stories that take place in New York City during the 1980s. She lives in Washington Heights with her husband, Phillip Margulies, and their two children.

HOLLIS SEAMON is the author of YA novel *Somebody Up There Hates You* (Algonquin Young Readers, 2013): Fall 2013 Kids' Indie Next List pick, 2014 Best Book for Young Adults from the American Library Association, and 2013 Best Teen Fiction from *Kirkus Reviews*. She is also the author of the short story collection *Corporeality* (Able Muse Press, 2013): a gold medal winner in the 2014 Independent Publishers Awards, and a finalist for Foreword Review's 2014 Book of the Year. She has published a previous collection of stories, *Body Work,* and a mystery novel, *Flesh*. A recipient of a fiction fellowship from the New York Foundation for the Arts, Seamon is Professor of English at the College of Saint Rose in Albany, NY, and also teaches for the MFA in Creative Writing Program of Fairfield University.

ADEL SOUTO—See page 96.

MARILYN L. TAYLOR, former Poet Laureate of the state of Wisconsin (2009 and 2010) and of the city of Milwaukee (2004 and 2005), is the author of six collections of poetry. Her award-winning poems and essays have appeared in many anthologies and journals, including *Poetry, The American Scholar, Able Muse, Measure,* Ted Kooser's *American Life in Poetry* column, and in the recent Random House anthology titled *Villanelles*. Currently a board member of the Council for Wisconsin Writers, Marilyn also served for five years as Contributing Editor and regular poetry columnist for *The Writer* magazine. She recently moved from Milwaukee to Madison, Wisconsin, where she continues to write and teach.

Gustavo Thomas—See page 107.

Anne-Marie Thompson's first book, *Audiation,* won the 2013 Donald Justice Poetry Prize. She works as a technical writer and musician in Columbia, Missouri.

N.S. Thompson lives outside Oxford, UK. He has contributed essays and poetry to *Able Muse* and many other publications in the UK and USA, including *Agenda, Ambit, Modern Poetry in Translation, New Walk, Stand,* and *The American Scholar.* His books include the verse epistle in rime royal *Letter to Auden* (Smokestack, 2010) and he has coedited a collection of fifteen cantos in ottava rima chronicling the lively adventures of a twenty-first century version of Byron's hero: *A Modern Don Juan: Cantos for these Times by Divers Hands* (Five Leaves, September 2014).

A workshop with Cathy Smith Bowers inspired Gail Tyson to write dreams forward as pantoums, and she enjoys the challenges of all poetic forms, from the meticulous minute to the fiendish sestina. As often as she can, she writes at the cabin in the East Tennessee mountains that she shares with her husband, Dick, and border collie, Maggie. Gail earned an MA from Stanford University's Creative Writing Program, and her work has appeared in *America* and *Still Point Arts Quarterly*. When she is not writing poems, fiction and creative nonfiction, she works as an educational marketing consultant.

Paul Verlaine (1844 – 1896), precursor of the Symbolists, composed ten volumes of lushly musical poetry replete with eroticism and subtle moods. His life was a tempestuous sequence of prosperity, poverty, Parisian café society, a violent affair with the young Rimbaud, two imprisonments for assault—including one on his mother—as well as failed business ventures and intervals of teaching in England.

Wendy Videlock—See page 139.

J. Preston Witt is from Flushing, Michigan. His fiction has appeared in *Ninth Letter Online* and *The New Guard* and is forthcoming in the Red76 anthology *Trainwreck.* He finished his MFA from The Ohio State University in May 2014 and is the founding editor of the education project PhoneFiction.

Able Muse – Print Edition

Able Muse – No. 16, Winter 2013
Jehanne Dubrow, featured poet | **Peter Svensson**, featured artist
978-1-927409-27-5
- With rachel hadas, marly youmans, r.s. gwynn, cheryl diane kidder, a.e. stallings, david mason, chrissy mason, peter byrne, rory waterman, and others

Able Muse – No. 15, Summer 2013
Greg Williamson, featured poet | **Clara Lieu**, featured artist
978-1-927409-21-3
- With dick allen, fred longworth, robert j. levy, haley hach, ilya lyashevsky, david mason, peter byrne, david caplan, stephen kampa, n.s. thompson, and others

Able Muse – No. 14, Winter 2012
Catherine Tufariello, featured poet | **Nicolas Evariste**, featured artist
978-1-927409-07-7
- With thomas carper, lorna knowles blake, richard wakefield, tony barnstone, len krisak, evelyn somers, gregory dowling, aaron poochigian, and others

Able Muse – No. 13, Summer 2012
Patricia Smith, featured poet | **Andrew Ponomarenko**, featured artist
978-1-927409-01-5
- With wendy videlock, jennifer reeser, richard wakefield, julie bruck, kim bridgford, brian culhane, reginald dwayne betts, and others

Able Muse – No.12, Winter 2011
David Mason, featured poet | **Alper Çukur**, featured artist
978-0-9865338-9-1
- With suzanne j. doyle, timothy murphy, gabriel spera, richard wakefield, lyn lifshin, amit majmudar, rachel bentley, david j. rothman, and others

Able Muse – No. 11, Summer 2011
Catharine Savage Brosman, featured poet | **Emily Leonne Bennett**, featured artist
978-0-9865338-5-3
- With david mason, andrew waterman, john drury, rachel hadas, brian culhane, emily laithauser, leslie monsour, traci chee, and other

Able Muse – No. 10, Inaugural Print Edition, Winter 2010
R.P. Lister, featured poet | **Massimo Sbrini**, featured artist
978-0-9865338-2-2
- With catherine tufariello, catharine savage brosman, leslie monsour, j. patrick lewis, kim bridgford, nancy lou canyon, john whitworth, peter filkins, and others

Details at www.AbleMuse.com

From RED HEN PRESS

SLICE OF MOON
Poems by Kim Dower
978-1-59709-971-4 • Tradepaper • 18.95
104 pages

Kim Dower's first book of poems, *Air Kissing on Mars*, was described by poet Thomas Lux as "a rare and astonishing first book...a kind of a miracle." The *Los Angeles Times* called it "sensual and evocative... poems that traverse the chaos of everyday life with a light touch that can turn ironic and edgy without you even noticing it. Some are lyrical snapshots of life's bittersweet moments, while others seamlessly combine humor and heartache." Now, in her second collection, *Slice of Moon*, Kim Dower retains her whimsical style while reaching deeper, writing—of love, longing, motherhood, vulnerability, death—with the same humor and accessibility of her earlier work, but with greater lyrical intensity, irony, and poignancy.

Praise for *Slice of Moon*

"The poems are bold and sexy and smart."
—Stephen Dunn, Pulitzer Prize-winning poet

"*Slice of Moon* is a dark chocolate fever dream of love, of mothers. Kim Dower dares you into the dark. You may find yourself lurking there."
—Erica Jong

"Kim Dower's remarkable first book, *Air Kissing on Mars*, was on fire. *Slice of Moon* burns even hotter, its flames rising even higher."
—Thomas Lux

Available from the Chicago Distribution Center
To place an order: (800) 621-2736 / www.redhen.org

INDEX

Symbols

2015 Pushcart Prize v

A

Able Muse Anthology ii
Able Muse Book Award v, vi, vii, ix, xvi, 192, 193, 198
Able Muse Press ii, vii, xvi
Able Muse - Print Edition 207
Able Muse Write Prize viii
Able Muse Write Prize for Fiction v, 43
Able Muse Write Prize for Poetry v, 58, 80, 127, 168
Accepting the Disaster 171
Allen, Dick v, xv
All the Wasted Beauty of the World vi, vii, 192
"A Moonwalk in a Cowboy Hat: An Interview by David Mason" 139
"An Interview by David Mason" 139
Apfeld, Bridget 130, 199
Appel, Jacob M. 187
"A Review of Jacob M. Appel, *Scouting for the Reaper*" 187
Art & Photography 96, 97, 98, 99, 107, 108, 109, 111, 112, 113, 114, 116, 117, 118
Asperity Street – Poems v, xv, 213
Austin, Peter vi, 26, 199
A Vertical Mile vii, 197
"A walker in Central Park" 108
"A Woman and Her Cat" 23

B

Bachelor Pad 171
Bad Fame – Poems 213
Baer, William 213
Balmain, Melissa vi, vii, xvi, 198
Bennett, Emily Leonne 207
Bentley, Roy 45, 199
Berlin, Eric v, xv, 80, 199
Berman, Ben vii, 196
Book Reviews 171, 187
Brosman, Catharine Savage v, 76, 78, 199, 207

C

"Calypso Calls on Penelope" 163
Campion, Peter vi, ix
Cantor, Michael vii, 196
"*Cartel pour le combat à cheval, en forme de balet*" 194
Caylor, Duane 164, 200
"Challenge for a Mounted Tournament in the Form of a Ballet" 55
Chandler, Catherine v, vii, xv, 168, 197, 200
"Cicero Comments" 164
"Claire" 60
"Cleopatra's Needle" 97
Coe, Terese 56, 200
Cohen, Michael v, 100, 200
Coles, Katharine v, 74, 200
Collins, Billy xvi
Compositions of the Dead Playing Flutes vii
Conelly, William 213
Corbett, Maryann vii
Corporeality vii, 196
"Costanza e Preziosa" xv, 58
Crawford, Robert W. 163, 201
Credo for the Checkout Line in Winter vii
"Crucible at Kronshtadt" 119
Çukur, Alper 207
Culwell, David xv
Cup vi, vii, 192

D

Danielson, Jonathan vi
"Darning the Wounded Tongue" vi, 4
De Canio, Frank 57, 201
"Departure" 76
Dirge for an Imaginary World vii, 198
"Discovery" xv, 168
Dobozy, Tamas v, vi, 11, 201
"Dogwatch" 88
Dowling, Gregory vi
Drury, John 213
Dubrow, Jehanne 207

E

Editorial v
"Eight Stories In Search of an Editor" 187
"Either They Were Human" 74
Embarking on Catastrophe – Poems v, xv, 213
Eratosphere iii
Essays 81, 100, 119, 178
Evariste, Nicolas 207
"Evil" v

F

Featured Artist 107
Featured Poet 139, 153
Featured Poetry 139, 153, 154, 155, 156, 157
"Femme et chatte" 195
Fiction 11, 27, 43, 60, 130, 158
"Figure near Sólfar" 112
"For Lack of What Is Found" xv, 80
French 24, 56, 194, 195
Furr, Derek v, 178, 201
Furtney, Diane v, 24, 201

G

Gioia, Dana iii
Goodman, D.R. vi, vii, 193
Grasser, J.P. 128, 202
Grasshopper: The Poetry of M A Griffiths vii
Greed: A Confession vi, vii, 193
Griffiths, Margaret Ann vii

Gwynn, R.S. 88, 202
"Gyroscope" 128

H

Haas, Barbara v, 119, 202
"Harvest" 2
Heaven from Steam vii
Heimat: A Poem 171
Hesiod vi
Hix, H.L. vi, viii
Hodge, Jan D. 213
House Music vii
Huffaker, Lisa 1, 202

I

Interviews 88
"In the Wind" 157
"Invocation" 155

J

"Joshua Mehigan, *Accepting the Disaster*" 171
Justice, Donald 81

K

Kampa, Stephen v, vi, 6, 171, 202
Kaufman, Ellen vii
Kennedy, X.J. ii, v, xvi
Kevorkian, Karen vi
Kim, Eugenia vi, viii, xv
Krisak, Len v, 41, 202
Kunst, Judith 9, 202

L

Lacare, Michael v, 60, 203
LaRue, Dorie deWitt 70, 203
Lehr, Quincy R. 171
Leithauser, Hailey v, 51, 52, 53, 54, 203
"Lesson One" xv, 43, 44
Lieu, Clara 207
Life in the Second Circle vii, 196
Light, Carol vii
"Like Nothing Ever Seen on Earth" 9

Lindner, April vii
Lines of Flight vii, 197
Lister, R.P. 207
Locey, Kathryn 72, 203
"Lorca in California" 81

M

Majmudar, Amit v, xv, 44
Mason, David v, 139, 203, 207
Mastroianni, Anthony 158, 203
McGovern, Martin v, 171, 203, 213
McLean, Susan 42, 203
Mehigan, Joshua 171
Merrin, Jeredith v, vi, vii, 47, 50, 192, 204
Midnight in Paris 158
Milbrodt, Teresa 25, 204
Miller, Scott M. v, xv, 58, 204

N

"National Monument of Scotland" 114
Nevertheless vii, 197
New and Recent Releases from Able Muse Press vii
Newman, Richard vi, vii, 192
"New Wine" 72

O

"One one line, one one foot" 109
"On the bridge" 113
Osen, Frank vii, 198
"Our Elizabeth, Walcott Mine" 178

P

Peacock, Molly v, xv
"Peggy's Cove BNW panorama" 111
Pepple, Alexander ii, v
Pierre de Ronsard 55, 56, 194, 204
Poetry 1, 2, 4, 6, 9, 23, 25, 40, 41, 42, 45, 47, 51, 53, 54, 55, 57, 70, 72, 74, 76, 78, 80, 127, 128, 129, 139, 154, 155, 157, 163, 168, 170, 195
Poetry Translation 23, 55, 195
Pollock, James 196

Ponomarenko, Andrew 207
Poochigian, Aaron vii, 197
Potvin, Kyle 40, 204
Pumpkin Chucking vii

Q

"Quincy R. Lehr, *Heimat: A Poem*" 171

R

Raab, Zara 129, 205
'Reading Donald Justice's "Lorca in California"' 81
Reeser, Jason Phillip 88, 205
"Ride the island" 99
Ridland, John 213
Riley, John vi
Rimbaud, Arthur v
"River II: Accidental Reflection" xv, 127
Rogers, William E. xv
Rosaler, Maxine v, 27, 205
"Rrribbit" 51
"R.S. Gwynn, Interviewed by Jason Reeser" 88

S

Sailing to Babylon vii, 196
Sbrini, Massimo 207
Scaer, Stephen vii
Scouting for the Reaper 187
Sea Level Rising – Poems 213
Seamon, Hollis v, vii, 187, 196, 205
"Sensō-ji During Sanja Matsuri" 118
Shipers, Carrie v, xv, 213
"Short-Timer" 42
Sinclair, Safiya xv
Sir Gawain and the Green Knight – Translation 213
Siskel, Callie vi
Slingshots and Love Plums – Poems 213
Slot, Andrea Witzke xv
Smith, Matthew Buckley vii, 198
Smith, Patricia 207
Soderling, Janice D. vi
"Sonnet" 170
Sorensen, Barbara Ellen vii

"Sour Grapes" 52
Southward, David xv
Souto, Adel v, 96, 205
"'Squirrels on Skis' Star Performer Dies" 45
Stallings, A.E. v
Steele, Timothy ii
Stephen Kampa, Bachelor Pad 171
Strange Borderlands - Poems vii, 196
"Sunny" 78
Svensson, Peter 207

T

Taking Shape – carmina figurata 213
Taylor, Marilyn L. v, xv, 127, 205
"The Burrowing Owl" 47
The Cosmic Purr vii, 197
The Dark Gnu and Other Poems vii
"The Egg" 116
"The Five Races of Man" v
"The Hangman's Song" 54
"The Hermit Convention" vi, 6
"The Passion of Jude" 25
"The Pharaoh Eagle Owl" 50
"The Place Where It Happened" 100
"The Sere, the Yellow Leaf" 129
"The Tire Swing of Death" vi, 11
"The Uncle" 27
"The Vigilantes" 154
This Bed Our Bodies Shaped vii
Thomas, Gustavo v, 106, 107
Thompson, Anne-Marie 170, 206
Thompson, N.S. v, 81, 206
"Three Reviews" 171
Times Square and Other Stories 213
"To My Children Reading My Poetry after I'm Gone" 40
"To the Young Muslim Woman in Full Hijab on the Motorcycle" 70

"Tough Customer" 57
"Trees in November" 41
"Triolet with Typewriter" 53
Tufariello, Catherine 207
"Twenty Years On" 26
Tyson, Gail vi, 2, 4, 206

U

Uncontested Grounds – Poems 213
Upshaw, Reagan vi

V

Vellum vi, vii, 193
Verlaine, Paul 23, 24, 195, 206
Videlock, Wendy v, vii, 138, 139, 153, 154, 155, 156, 157, 197, 206, 213
Virtue, Big as Sin vii, 198

W

"Wake" 1
Wakefield, Richard vii, 197
Walking in on People vi, vii, xvi, 198
"Walk on by" 98
"Water Deep, Cold" 130
"Water Street (Osaka)" 117
"What the Sculptor Said" 156
White, Gail v, xv, 213
Williamson, Greg 207
Witt, J. Preston v, xv, 43, 44, 206
Woodard, Chelsea vi, vii, 193
Wright, Rob vi
Write Prize for Fiction vi
Write Prize for Poetry vi

Y

Yezzi, David xvi

COMING SOON
2014 / 2015
from

Able Muse Press

William Baer, *Times Square and Other Stories*

William Conelly, *Uncontested Grounds – Poems*

John Drury, *Sea Level Rising – Poems*

Martin McGovern, *Bad Fame – Poems*

Wendy Videlock, *Slingshots and Love Plums – Poems*

Carrie Shipers, *Embarking on Catastrophe – Poems*

Gail White, *Asperity Street – Poems*

Jan D. Hodge, *Taking Shape – carmina figurata*

John Ridland, *Sir Gawain and the Green Knight – Translation*

MORE INFORMATION AVAILABLE AT

www.AbleMusePress.com

www.ingramcontent.com/pod-product-compliance
Lightning Source LLC
Chambersburg PA
CBHW081847170426
43199CB00018B/2839